Practical Engine Swapping

By John Thawley

Fourth Revised Edition

Editor	Steve Smith
Associate Editor	Georgiann Smith

Revised August 1987

Published by

Steve Smith Autosports

P.O. Box 11631, Santa Ana, CA 92711

Foreword

Handing out thanks for help on a book like this is difficult—not because we are reluctant to offer it, but because we don't know where to start or stop. In the several years we have had the opportunity to write "Swap Talk" for **Popular Hot Rodding**, our "agony of the month" came when we finished the column at two in the morning each month and still saw a pile of letters going unanswered. This book was predicated on the belief there are thousands of guys out there wanting something a little different in the way of transportation—an engine swap—and don't know quite how to go about it in a practical manner. Engine swappers like Andy Herbert, Steve Chase and Dick Goold helped clear the air on a lot of questions. Their guidance, help and patience is greatly appreciated. Manufacturers, street rodders, off roaders and a long suffering patient family offered encouragement and we thank all of you for the contribution.

John Thawley

The Cover: Dick Goold of Galt, California makes final adjustments before installing a '74 Cadillac engine and transmission into his '55 Chevy truck. The truck is also equipped with a Blazer 12 bolt rear axle. Photo by the author.

Table Of Contents

Why Swap?

Putting the engine from one car or truck into another vehicle really didn't get any publicity until California hot rodders started doing "their thing" in the late thirties. Part of their thing was to put big engines in light cars and race—on tracks and on streets. Now, hot rodding in various forms is a multi-million dollar business. Thousands of enthusiasts are involved and various aspects of the sport, such as drag racing, draw huge crowds. Engine swapping is still part of the scene, for competition and—increasingly—for every day use. But just for a moment we should give a tip of the hat to the unknown soul performing the first engine swap. We'll bet the swap came very early in the history of the automobile—the early twenties, maybe even earlier. There were probably two disabled vehicles involved. Perhaps one had rolled over and the other suffered a cracked block in the dead of winter. Cold Yankee logic said one running car could be made from two disabled cars. Since necessity really is the mother of invention, we have to believe that first swap was done in order to provide someone with transportation—not to terrorize the neighborhood with a fire belching, tire smoking roadster.

This book is concerned with presenting solid information on engine swapping in three general areas—transportation, "toy" and competition. Many times a transportation and toy swap can be combined; at other times a toy swap and a competition swap can be combined. But in the real world of today you can forget about having a transportation and competition swap in one car.

A competition swap, pure and simple. A Ford DOHC 427 in an early Thunderbird built for drag racing.

Installing a modern V8 in any small car is done to create a "toy" which is capable of rather startling performance on the street. Normally this sort of swap involves far more work than most engine swappers bargain for.

Since we will be referring to these three areas of swapping throughout the book, each area should be defined.

TRANSPORTATION

By far there is more interest in performing an engine swap to provide a reliable, low cost way of getting to work each day than any other reason. The swap might not work out that way—but the intent was there. With the ever-rising cost of cars and light trucks there is even more reason to consider engine swapping now than ten years ago. The transportation swap must be reliable, reasonable in cost and provide the driver with most, if not all, the driving comforts available before the swap took place. If you had air conditioning and power steering before the swap, why not have it after the swap? A swap performed for basic transportation usually requires a lot of planning and cold thinking if it is to be reliable and low cost. The heart must give way to the head. For example, if your 1962 Chevy sedan has a terminal death rattle under the hood you might consider installing another engine—like the big block Ford sitting on your garage floor. After all, the engine is in very good condition and is complete except for the alternator and starter. The heart might be saying "yes", but hopefully you will listen to your brain when it says "no." This swap will be time consuming and in the end be costly. It could be reliable, but we'd bet with the limited skills of most back yard swappers it won't be. A transportation swap should be sensible. This one doesn't fall in that category. If you truly want another

engine in that Chevy, trade the Ford engine for another Chevy engine in better shape than the one you're now driving. Since this is a bolt-in swap, it will be as reliable as the hardware—almost totally unrelated to your mechanical skills. Compared to installing the Ford in the Chevy, installing the Chevy engine in the Chevy will be quick and easy. Minor problems that might come up can be solved by a visit to a wrecking yard, parts store or dealership parts counter. Never lose sight of the fact that mere possession of some unrelated automotive hardware rarely lends itself to a good transportation swap. Think long and hard before lighting the torch for a transportation swap.

A more practical toy that bridges the gap towards dependable transportation is a small block Chevy in the back seat area of a late Corvair via a Crown or Kelmark engine swap kit.

TOY

Wives and mothers are quick to point out the only difference between men and boys is the cost of their toys—and we all know how much fun toys are. An engine swap done on the premise of having a good time with the end result is rewarding in many ways. To a great extent we simply don't care what the swap costs. If we are not depending on the toy to get us to work Monday morning, we are not pressed for time in doing the

Large V8 engines and pickups are naturals for the swap scene and provide smooth dependable power to thousands of owners. This is a late Buick in a '56 Ford pickup.

installation. If our ego dictates that we have a big block Chevy in an early Ford pickup, then we can solve problems in stride. This is all part of the fun. Thousands of swaps wind up being a very good combination of toy and transportation. In many cases they are far more reliable, lower in cost and certainly more fun to drive than anything you'll find in a dealer's show room. You should realize there are toys and there are toys. A big block Chevy in an early Ford truck is what we'd call a

transportation toy. A big block Chevy in an MG is a toy for the sake of a toy. Just to get this swap to the stage of making it around the block under its own power will be a challenge. A considerable amount of time, labor and skill is involved and in the end the result will be an overheating, ill-handling beast that is noisy, and hard to stop. The owner will be the talk of the neighborhood and maybe the local police department because this thing will run like a scalded ape—at least for a while. For better or for worse, this is a toy. There are all kinds.

COMPETITION

Engine swapping in a race car can run the gamut from installing a small block Chevy in a Formula A chassis originally set up for a small block Ford to installing a big block Chevy in a Vega for drag racing. A swap for competition should not be confused with a swap as a toy and certainly it bears no resemblance to a swap for transportation. There are very strict rules in all racing associations regarding not only what engines may be used with what chassis, but how the engine may be placed in the chassis. Basically a

A big block Chevy was an easy swap for this early Chevy and provides the owner with unusual daily transportation.

competition swap is concerned with only two things—passing tachnical inspection and winning races. In the heady world of racing, money takes a back seat in swap strategy and no one is concerned with emission control hardware or where to mount the air conditioning compressor. The swap must be reliable and it must lend itself to winning.

Straight eight Packard gets replaced with late model V8 to provide long lasting service for a big, heavy road car capable of keeping up with today's flow of traffic . . . at far less money than a new car.

Before You Start

Of the thousands of engine swaps done each year, it is safe to assume that several hundred of them are failures. The swap may never be completed for any number of reasons and eventually the eyesore and remainder of the mechanical miscarriage is hauled off to a wrecking yard. Other swaps are completed and the car is driven for a while. Then problems arise which cannot be solved by the owner and the car winds up at the end of a rope being towed to the local garage so a mechanic can fix whatever is wrong. Maybe he can solve the problems and turn the swap into a success—for a certain number of greenbacks. Maybe the mechanic will tell you his bill will be five times what the car will be worth after he fixes it.

Little is said of engine swap failures. We all have our pride and we are reluctant to admit our failures. For most of us they are uncomfortable topics of conversation. Before starting a swap you should be aware it can be a failure. Never lose sight of that grim prospect while planning a swap and this can go a long way towards making the swap a success.

HOW DO YOU SEE THE FINISHED PRODUCT?

On previous pages we put engine swapping into three classifications and before you start a swap you should place your proposal into one of those little areas and make a cold assessment of how the swap will turn out, based on everything you can think of which will affect the swap. Let's take a closer look at swapping in this light.

Experience—Don't let your pride in the area of experience lead you down the primrose path of engine swapping. Just how familiar are you with automotive hardware? I don't mean the kind of familiarity you get by reading car magazines. I mean the kind of experience you get from laying on a creeper on a cold garage floor wrestling with a rusty tailpipe and muffler. Have you ever bloodied your knuckles trying to get a fuel pump off? Have you ever gone through the simple job of installing a high performance intake manifold on an engine only to find out it doesn't fit quite right and you've got to make it fit—or put the stock manifold back on? Ever installed a set of headers, a new clutch or removed a radiator to have it

This small block Ford in a Jaguar now looks like it was factory installed, but the amount of time, skill and money involved is staggering. Even a professional in a hurry could botch a swap as involved as this. Look before you leap—or cut—or ruin a car.

Although building a Chevy-powered early Ford hot rod may appear very straightforward here, the fact is that a lot of welding and fabricating have been done just to get the chassis to this point. Consider where you'll store the body if you plan to remove it.

boiled out? Have you ever removed an engine from a car, had it rebuilt and then reinstalled it in the car? If you have actually done some of these things—or all of them in addition to others, then you might be able to do an engine swap. If your answer to all of the above is along the lines you've never actually worked on a car but you know you could do an engine swap, my advice is to be very careful in choosing the first swap you attempt. Actual mechanical experience is impossible to beat when you run headlong into a real problem in the swap. Basic automotive experience is the single most important thing you can have in your favor when doing an engine swap. Be honest with yourself when making this assessment—or be miserable every step of the way in the swap.

Skills—In the case of engine swapping, skills are normally tied directly to experience. Do you know

a little about metal working? When you drill a hole does it turn out round, or oval? Don't laugh. When you measure a piece of steel and cut it with a hacksaw, does it fit like you wanted it to? Or do you have to cut another piece and another. If you have a feel for metal working and have done some fabrication then you most likely will be able to handle a swap—but not all swaps.

Tools—You wouldn't try to build a wooden workbench without a hammer, saw and some other related wood working tools, and you shouldn't try to do an engine swap without a pretty fair collection of automotive tools—wrenches, screwdrivers and the like. In addition to the normal assortment of hand tools you should have, or know where you can get, some special tools. Rental firms can supply you with a portable engine hoist and maybe even a floor jack which comes in

Notching a shock tower is sometimes necessary when big engines go in little cars. In all honesty, can you do the job in a workmanlike manner so the integrity and rigidity of the structure is maintained?

Rebuilding the firewall in this swap was easy; completely rebuilding and relocating the entire wiper mechanism cost about as much as the rest of the swap!

very handy on most swaps. A small assortment of wooden blocks, and crowbars or pieces of pipe will also come in handy when you are trying to move a four hundred pound engine a couple of inches.

On some swaps you'll need an arc welder. These can also be rented. If you have never used one before, I'd suggest that you not practice on an engine swap. Check the yellow pages for firms having a portable welding rig. For a fee they'll come to your garage or front yard and do the welding for you. A gas welder is also very handy for most swaps. Even if you don't use it for welding, they are mighty handy for heating a bracket or panel that needs a little bending. There are swaps where a cutting torch is a necessity. Here again, a portable welding rig can take care of cutting as well as welding, but if you have to call a

Installing a small block Chevy in some of the mini-trucks can involve removing most of the firewall. This can take about 15 minutes with a torch or panel cutter. Depending on your skill and experience, rebuilding a firewall can take a full day or a full week.

Before starting with your swap, make a very careful assessment as to how you see the finished project—a racer, a toy or a transportation vehicle. This Volvo is now powered by a Toyota.

welder to your home several times during the course of a swap your final engine swap bill will look like the national debt.

Space—You don't need much space if you know how to use it. I've done swaps in driveways—mainly because the single car garage was so cluttered it would take more time to get the car inside than it would to do the engine swap outside. The time you have to use the space should be considered. An apartment landlord might get a little on the "lordy" side if you shed the front sheet metal off your car and leave it scattered around for three months while you diddle on the swap for three hours a week. If it is your driveway at your house with your car involved then normally you have to deal only with your wife. Write your own chapter on that subject. There are also small commercial warehouses and storage yards where you can perform the work if there is not enough space around the home.

Time—For the amateur an engine swap will normally take about four times longer than he figures it will. So make your estimate and multi-ply by four. Time is of great importance in some swaps and of no consequence in others. If you sneak off work early some Friday afternoon to get a head start on a weekend swap you plan on driving to work Monday morning, then time is very important, and I want to wish you a lot of luck on the project. Some swaps can be so time consuming and overbearing with problem after problem that the owner loses interest and finally stops all work on the project. The swap then becomes a failure—and an albatross—a mechanically crippled, dust covered monster. If this is a toy and the toy is not in your way, then an unfinished swap may be only a mild irritation. If the swap involves your only means of transportation—and you need transportation, the irritation level increases considerably.

Money—You'll need some. Just how much, I don't know. Every swap is a little different. At the back of the book there is a little cost guide which breaks down an engine swap. Some of the items will apply to your swap; some won't. I'd suggest using this form to estimate costs of the swap you

Most anything in the way of equipment can now be rented—such as an engine hoist like this.

contemplate as thoroughly as you can. Let's say you come up with an estimate of $600. Take one third of that amount—$200—and add it to your estimate. Plan on that being the total, out-the-door running, cost of the swap. Live with that figure; then if you come in under that total with a successful swap you can tell everyone how much you saved and feel double good about the swap.

At this point you may be thinking—this book is aimed against swapping. Hardly. A swap can be fun, neat, low cost, practical and reliable. But the very best way I know of insuring that, is to assess each project honestly and realistically. Go back to the question we posed—how do you see the finished project. Be honest now.

Will It Fit?

In any contemplation of any engine swap the first question is always "Will it fit?" Once and for all, I will answer the question. Yes. It will fit. No matter what car is involved or what engine is under consideration, the answer will always be: yes, it will fit. The answer is correct but the question is the wrong one to ask or contemplate. What you really want to know is, what will have to be done to get the engine into the car and make it run; and is it practical? As we shall soon discover, the question of what is practical for you is the only real question to be answered regarding any swap.

What is practical for you? Never lose sight of that question; answer it honestly and you will be a successful engine swapper. Reflections of people never considering that point is a typical question to a hot rodding magazine:

Dear Sir:

Can you put a Chrysler hemi in a Honda Civic? Is this a practical swap?

Yours truly,

Hank Gofast

Dear Mr. Engineswapperfeller:

Yes, you can put a Chrysler hemi in a Honda Civic. Yes, this is a practical swap if you never intend to drive the car. With enough time and money there are a number of craftsmen who could make a hemi in a Honda an outstanding swap for the show circuit. Tastefully accented with chrome, plenty of annodized aluminum and a smokey pearl paint job with candy apple flames, this would be a mind blower at car shows and in the long run you might not only regain the cost of the swap, but make a profit by continuously leasing the car out for display purposes.

Yours truly,

Joe Weldingrod

Get the point? The answer is always "yesitwillfit." The question is always "isitpracticalforyou?" Tune your thinking to what the finished product will be and is it practical for you to solve the problems in order to finish the project.

Generally speaking, it is easier to swap within a "family" of cars than it is to crossbreed chassis and engine. By this we mean that, for the

Use scraps of steel, straight edges and bailing wire to center and level engine in the vehicle. Time and patience spent at this point eliminates all kinds of problems later.

After engine has been shoved back as far as it needs to go, it must be leveled laterally. A mechanic's level rests on the manifold mating surface of the block to accomplish this.

When a firewall must be cut to properly locate engine, it is wise to cut the hole large enough for the bare block only in the first step.

(Below) After the block has been located and the mounts fabricated, the firewall opening can be enlarged. Note that a radiator has been dropped in place in order to determine fan clearance.

moment, think in terms of putting a Chevy engine in a Chevy, Ford engine in a Ford and a Chrysler engine in a Chrysler-built car—and so on. There are exceptions to this line of thinking and in time we'll cover this. For a moment, let us assume you have a '68 Camaro. It is equipped with a six cylinder engine and Powerglide. The engine is very tired and will soon need rebuilding. You are thinking about swapping engines instead of rebuilding the old one. You would like to have more horsepower and you think a V8 would be the answer. So far you are on the right track. Any small block Chevy—from 1958 on up—will bolt in place using stock Chevy parts. Any big block Chevy—396, 402, 427 or 454 will do the same thing. You see, both small and large block Chevy engines will bolt in with factory parts because the factory planned it that way. A swap such as this is truly a weekend job if you have acquired every piece of factory hardware needed before ever pulling the six banger out. To point out that this is a practical swap may be like telling you that snow is cold, but as this is written I know of two early Camaros that may never be driven again because one owner is attempting to install a big block Ford and a four speed transmission in his and the other chap is bound and determined to have the only

This is the size opening you'll most likely encounter when trying to put any full size V8 and automatic into a mini-pickup. This is a small block Chevy and Turbo 350 in a Datsun.

streetable Chrysler Hemi powered Camaro in the country.

In our example of Chevy into Chevy, the factors of cost, time, skill and experience necessary to complete the job are held to an absolute minimum. Naturally, there are limits to swapping within a family of engines and chassis. Installing a big block Chevy in a Vega or Monza is practical only if it is to be used in all out drag racing. But, in these days of racing expertise and technology, the finished product of big block in a Vega or Monza can hardly be called a car. It is an expensive mechanism designed for the sole purpose of racing similar mechanisms.

If swapping within a family of engines and cars does not fit your plans, consider swapping an engine of the same basic size, shape and displacement as what you now have under the hood. To illustrate this line of thinking let us assume for the moment you have an MG TD. You love the car and hate the engine and want to swap for something more modern in design. A later MG engine is out of the question since you live in East Overshoe, Montana, and your MG is the only example of the species in the state—dead or alive. In a case such as this you might start doing some serious thinking about an engine and transmission from a Toyota, Datsun, Opel, Colt or Fiat.

The third general area of picking the right engine for your particular car or truck is to pick a swap combination having great popularity due to the fact complete aftermarket swap kits are available. Most all of the swaps in this category are several years old and continue to be popular because they are practical and easy for the amateur. The manufacturer of the swap kit is well

aware most engine swappers have limited skills, experience and patience. Thus the hardware is designed to solve problems as straightforward as possible. For example, Advance Adapters Inc. makes every piece of hardware necessary to install a small block Chevy into a Toyota Land Cruiser. This particular swap is so popular Advance makes variations of the kit which allow a Turbo Hydro 400, Muncie 4 speed or stock Toyota transmission to be used. The nit-picking small items normally having to be fabricated in a swap of this kind are included in this kit such as a bracket which allows the Toyota alternator to be bolted to the Chevy

Short lengths of boards come in very handy when determining preliminary engine placement.

(Left) Even professional engine swappers rely on short hydraulic jacks to move heavy components around. (Above) The structural integrity of the body begins to suffer when large sections are removed from the cowl and firewall.

engine without pain or strain. Obviously this all adds up to a practical swap situation for the amateur.

There are few kits available as complete as the example just given. The vast majority of kits consist of frame mounts, transmission crossmembers and sometimes headers designed specifically to solve a clearance problem. These kits are very popular. For some they create problems, for others they solve problems. For the guy who has overestimated his experience and skills, the problems are created because he believes the kit will solve all of his problems—and they don't. For the swapper who realizes the kit solves the problem of

Sheet metal alterations can get extensive—and expensive—when big engines are shoved into small vehicles. This might be more work than you want.

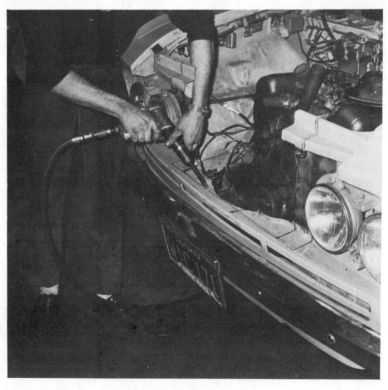

When large sections of sheet metal are grafted back on to a body, care must be taken when welding to avoid warpage of the existing structure.

how and where to mount the engine, and solve the exhaust clearance problem with the steering box, and that he will be on his own for the rest of the details, this type of kit works out fine. Major fabrication jobs are eliminated and time is saved which can now be devoted to the small but important details necessary to complete the job. Again the question—is it practical for you?

The lack of aftermarket engine swap hardware does not mean a particular swap is not practical; it could mean it is simply lacking in popularity. Looking at it from the manufacturer's side, why would you tool up and make 500 or 5000 engine mount kits to install a big block wedge Chrysler in '54-'56 Ford pickups when most owners of these trucks want small block Chevys and Fords? In the case of the Chrysler in the Ford truck, we have a swap lacking in popularity that might be very practical for an individual having the skills and experience to tackle the job with confidence. Back to the old question: what is practical for you?

WHY WE ARE WHERE WE ARE IN SWAPPING

An abbreviated history lesson is in order if you are reasonably new to the swap scene. Perhaps this will serve to answer some quesions you hadn't even thought of yet! History of any kind has a sly way of doing that. All through the thirties, forties and part of the fifties, the vast majority of cars built in this country used some sort of torque tube drive. In rough and dirty terms this means the driveshaft between the transmission and the rear axle was enclosed. In this system there are two mechanical links between transmission and rear axle—the driveshaft and the tube surrounding it (making up the torque tube). This system is now considered archaic. In order to pull a clutch or transmission either the engine or rear axle assembly had to be removed from the car. The amount of unsprung weight was great when compared to that of an open driveline system.

Many early cars and trucks achieved frame rigidity with an X-member between the frame rails. Some of this must be cut away to install larger, newer engines. Some sort of structure should be used to replace the part of the X-member needing to be removed.

The entire front sub-frame on this Jaguar roadster has been replaced in order to provide room for a small block V8. This is a job for an expert fabricator only since the alignment and placement of the front suspension and steering is involved.

Here's an excellent example of replacing an old X-member with a new one to retain structural rigidity.

More parts were needed than with an open drive-line. We could go on.

Engine swaps "in the old days" involving torque tube drive-equipped chassis used an adapter between the new engine and the existing transmission. The use of the adapter plate between engine and transmission came into full bloom with the advent of the overhead valve V8 of the fifties. The simple solution to installing one of the new engines into the early chassis was an adapter plate made of cast aluminum which was sandwiched between engine and transmission. More often than not this was done while a floor jack supported the engine between the frame rails. Once the engine and transmission were mated, the jack lowered the engine down as low as possible while still providing clearance with various appendages such as front suspension members known as wishbones. At this point engine mounts were fabricated and the swap was well on its way. This was the rule of the day in engine swapping. The method was expedient and generally successful. From the outset, though, there were problems. They were solved in time by Detroit engineers and evolution; not by hot rodders.

The use of an adapter plate between an existing transmission and engine means the location of the transmission dictates the position of the engine in the chassis. In some of the early swaps this didn't matter much; in others it did. If the location of the transmission placed the new engine too far forward or excessively high in the chassis the swap might be likened unto a tail wagging the dog instead of vice versa.

Adapter plates flourished because it was the simple, straightforward method of installing a late model engine into a torque tube chassis. There were and are disadvantages to this method of swapping, though, and this you should know about. We have already mentioned one. The location of the transmission in the car determines the location of the new engine. If this shoved the engine upward or forward, the handling and braking of the car could be severly affected. Secondly, adapting a newer engine to an existing transmission and rear axle caused some serious reliability problems—dependant mainly on how the car was driven. Think about it—a transmission and rear axle designed to accept an 85 horsepower engine were now being bolted up to engines having 200 horsepower—or more. Axles broke and teeth were sheared off gears like a bucktooth farmer going through an ear of corn. Engine swappers of the day accepted all of this as part of the game; they didn't necessarily like replacing broken parts all of the time but they didn't have much choice. Swaps involving a new engine and the transmission designed for it were few and far between. The problem here was how to mate the back of the new transmission to the front of the old torque tube. Machine work was required—and this was out of the question for most individuals. Even if someone went to the trouble and expense of adapting the new transmission to the old torque tube, the old axle remained

as the weak link in the drivetrain. Installing a later rear axle in most of the older cars was really a chore since many of the cars had transverse springs in the rear, while the later, stronger axles were built to mate with semi-elliptical springs. A lot of cutting and welding was required in a day when small, reasonable cost welders were not available for home use.

By the mid-fifties most of the torque tubes were gone and more and more swaps were being done. And they were done with an engine and transmission combination instead of an engine and adapter. A wide variety of adapter plate hardware is still being sold and used in hundreds of swaps every year. For a great number of swaps they are practical and ideal. Using an adapter can make the difference between an individual doing a swap and not doing one, so they still have their place in the swap scene. Their place is simply not as large as it once was. As this book progresses, we'll get deeper into the use of adapters—but hopefully, this sketch of swap history will show why there is more than one way to put a small block Chevy in a '40 Ford, or whatever the case may be.

MEASURE IT!!

Let us assume for a moment that one fine morning you decide to explore the possibility of putting a small block Belchfire into a Pinto. You should approach the project by rereading the previous sentence. Note we did not say you were going to do the swap—just explore the possibility. Begin by popping the hood open and measuring the length, width and depth of the engine compartment. Note such things as the placement of

This is an increasingly common configuration of small block Chevy, Model A frame and body and late Jaguar suspension. Note placement of alternator to allow stock hood to be closed.

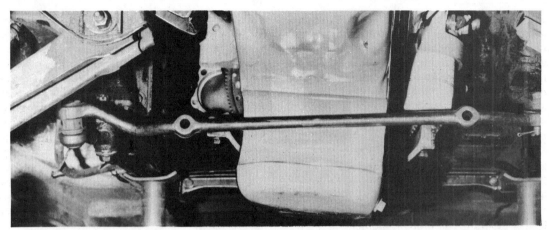

Altering an oil pan is a fairly common method of providing clearance with some steering mechanisms. Note that pan has been made deeper to make up for the capacity lost by the deep notch.

the steering box, steering linkage, and crossmember. Make a little drawing of the engine compartment and write in all of the measurements. Go to the nearest wrecking yard and measure a small block Belchfire engine. Make a front and side drawing of the engine just as we have done here and write in all of the measurements. In addition to the measurements we have given you in the chart, measure the diameter of the front crank dampner or crank pulley—whichever is largest. Also measure from the center of the crank to the top of the air cleaner.

Now you can transfer these dimensions of the eingine into your engine compartment without having to buy an engine, without having to pull the engine now in the car and without butchering up the entire front of the car trying to make something fit where it doesn't belong. Doing all of this measuring will not insure the swap will be easy even if your figures say the engine will fit—but it will hopefully keep you from getting in over your head in a swap.

You want to install the engine as low and as far to the rear as possible for the best in handling. Obviously, there are practical considerations. With your drawings and measurements in hand you can now determine a number of important items. Will the radiator have to be moved? Will the firewall have to be cut? Will the shock towers have to be notched? Will the oil pan hit the crossmember or any of the steering? If the engine will fit, can the stock exhaust manifolds be used or will special headers have to be fabricated?

Let us assume there is a crossmember of some sort at the front of the engine compartment and you've determined by your measurements that the crank pulley will be directly over this item. The pulley, and thus the engine, will have to be placed high enough in the compartment to allow a fan belt to be placed on the pulley. With this in mind, will you now have to cut a hole in the hood to accomodate the air cleaner?

Take plenty of time to do all of this. More than anything else, this measuring serves to eliminate surprises later on. After you have measured everything three times and made some determinations as to what will have to be done and what won't be needed you must now coldly decide if the swap is practical **for you**! Make an assessment of your time, space, experience, tools, and money and weigh all of this against the total project. The master craftsman with plenty of time and tools but short on cash can take care of a swap with little problem, but the man with money and no time or experience will simply never get around to finishing the job. Measure it—then make a judgement as to where you stand.

Our engine specification chart was designed to let you do a little arm chair engineering on your proposed swap without spending a lot of time or effort. However, when you get serious about the swap, go to a wrecking yard and do your own

(Above) Ideally, the exhaust manifold should come no closer to the steering box than ½-inch. Grease within a steering box can get very hot and cause premature rupture of the seals.

(Right) There should be sufficient clearance everywhere to perform routine maintenance to the car and engine without making it a major operation. Getting the drive belt on this air conditioning compressor should be fun.

measuring. The same basic engine will vary from year to year and even from one vehicle to another within the same year. Going by our chart we could get you into trouble by unintentionally giving you the "wrong" dimension. Perhaps we measured a small block Chevy having a short shaft water pump and the engine you buy is equipped with a long shaft pump. You hadn't counted on that—and to make matters worse you didn't know about the short shaft pump so you wind up moving the radiator forward which, for you, turns out to be more of a job than the rest of the swap. Do your own measuring. Make your own determination about what will need to be done to make the engine fit.

Determine where the centerline of the crank will be in your chassis and start figuring out where everything else will fall. Based on your measurements will the alternator hit the hood? Will the starter hit the steering box? Does the oil pan sump interfere with some of the steering linkage? Exhaust manifold or header clearance is critical in many of today's swaps. Will this problem cause you grief? Methodically make a list of the problems you think you will have. All of these—and other—problems in swapping are routinely solved in thousands of swaps each year. That's not the point though. The point is that this is your swap—with your car, your time and your money. You are the guy that had better give it all some serious thought before getting in over your head.

A far more sanitary approach here would have been to leave the frame brace intact and use a remote oil filter mount.

Chrysler-built V8's create oil filter clearance problems in most frames due to the forward placement of the filter.

MAINTAIN THE STRUCTURE

To understand why a crossmember is in a particular location you must understand that "bean counters" in Detroit have a heavy hand in all that gets to the production stage. Long before your car was ever built, it was picked apart on the drawing board by some pretty sharp characters trying to figure out how to save on manufacturing costs. They probably wanted to know if the

crossmember could be eliminated altogether; since the answer was no, they then wanted to know if the item could serve two or more functions—locate some suspension and the radiator. At the same time this was going on, someone was asking if the item could be made less complex and lighter—thus lower in cost. By the time that crossmember gets off the drawing board, out of the proving grounds, out of engineering and past the hands of the bean counters you can figure just about every aspect of that crossmember has been justified. For this reason modifying structural members of a chassis during the course of an

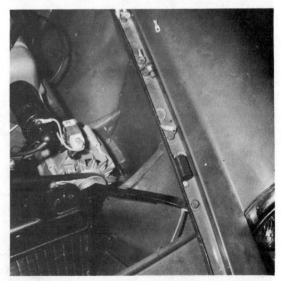

Clearance for this alternator was provided by cutting a portion of the inner fender panel away and then grafting in new metal with pop rivets. Also note the simple, but effective radiator brace.

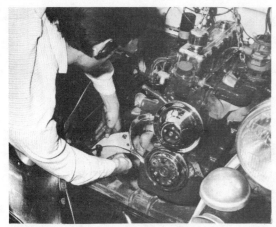

Once the engine is where you want it in the chassis, simple cardboard templates can be used to determine size and shape of mounts. With accurate templates, a local welding shop can fabricate mounts.

engine swap should not be taken lightly. In the early days of hot rodding, structural failure in frames and crossmembers was quite common. The engine was simply too much for the chassis. Nowdays this problem is rare—but it can still happen when the integrity of the structure is disturbed. What looks like an inner fender panel to you might actually be a stressed piece of sheet metal upon which the suspension depends for alignment. Think before you light up, and I'm not speaking of cigarettes. Structural integrity must always be considered when you are doing preliminary measuring.

IS IT WORTH IT—IN DOLLARS AND SENSE

You have now measured engines and engine compartments six ways from sundown and have determined the engine will fit and you are capable of doing the job. Where do you start? Start with the title of this book. Note that the word PRACTI-CAL is in the title. Use that one word as a yardstick to measure how you see the finished product. Only you can do that.

If you are facing a major engine overhaul on that six banger and want more performance than it will deliver once the job is complete, then an engine swap should certainly be considered. We've seen swaps where hundreds of dollars were saved by swapping instead of rebuilding. It can be done. If cost is important to you then you should spend some time shopping for engines, and pricing hardware needed to complete the job. Do not regard the dollar side of a swap lightly. At this point you can walk away from the proposed swap without a loss—you might not be able to do that later on.

The sense side of a swap is just as important. Consider everything you can think of—your experience, time, space, tools, interest in the project, and options you have. Options? Yup. If you are bound and determined to have a Cadillac engine in your Chevy pickup, it might make far more sense to have someone else do the swap for you. That is an option. Think about it.

EDUCATION—A LOW COST KEY TO SUCCESS

Before buying an engine and beginning a swap, educate yourself on all of the particulars of your swap. Some of this could be classified as armchair engineering and some of it won't be. Factory service manuals, old sales literature and maga-

If you don't have the experience and facilities to fabricate a tunnel for the new transmission, a sheet metal shop can help out after you have the vehicle in running condition.

When a complete running gear change is underway—engine, trans and rear axle—it often goes much more quickly if major sections of the body are removed.

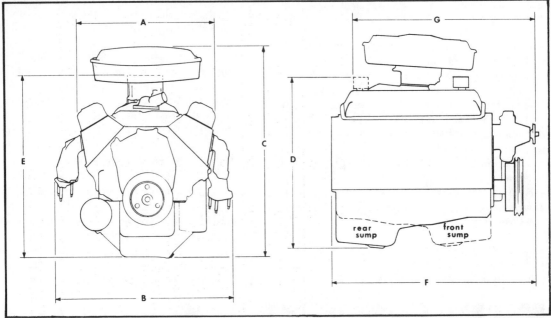

rear sump

front sump

The letters A through G shown on these two drawings indicate dimensions for popular engines as given in the chart on page 23.

zines might tell you that for your purposes a certain year 289 Ford is better than another. Chances are, though, that only visits to a wrecking yard or a dealership parts counter will tell you how many different oil pans are available for the engine. In other words you could save yourself a lot of hassle and money if you knew the small block V8 used in a Bronco uses a different pan than the one used in passenger cars. This piece of information alone could literally make or break a swap.

Fortunately for all of us dyed in the wool swappers, the most popular engines for swapping are those that are plentiful, reasonable in cost and are subtly changed by the factory from year to year. Changing the shape of the oil pan on an engine means nothing if you are buying an engine on a dealer's showroom floor—surrounded by an all new car. The shape of an oil pan can mean everything in certain swaps. Talk to parts men at the dealership. Tell them what you have in mind. Ask specific quesions. Listen to the answers. If they are vague, check another parts man at another dealership. Make yourself known at a wrecking yard or two. Take measurements, make drawings, ask specific questions and listen. There are guys all over the country working in wrecking yards and dealerships that can supply you with information about engine swapping that will never appear in print. Educate yourself; find a teacher.

ENGINE	CID	OIL SUMP (stock)	STARTER	WEIGHT	A	B	C	D	E	F	G
American Motors 6	232/258	rear	left	525	24	24	29	35	26	30	25
American Motors V8	304/360/401	rear	right	540	21½	25½	29½	29¼	28	28¾	21½
Buick V6	196/231/252	middle	right	370	24	26	28½	23	25½	23	21½
Buick V8	350	rear	right	450	23	28½	28½	30½	25½	29	21½
Buick V8	430/455	middle	left	600	23	28	30	30	27	29	22
Chevy 4	153	front	right	350	16	23½	28	23½	25½	22½	24
Chevy/Pontiac Olds/Buick 6	250	rear	right	410	16	23½	28	32½	25½	30½	24
Chevy V8	265/283/302 307/350/400	rear	right	550	19½	26	27	27	25	26½	25
Chevy V8	396/402/427 454	rear	right	625	22	27	33	30½	29½	30½	23½
Ford 6	144/250	front	right	400	17	17	28	31	26	29	24
Ford 6	240/300	front	right	400	13	13	28	32	26	30	24
Ford V8	260/289/302 351	front	right	460	20	22	27	29	25	29	27
Ford V8	332/352/390 410/428	front	right	625	23	27	32	32	30	32	30
MoPar 6	170/198/225	front	right	475	24	30	26	31½	22	30	29½
MoPar V8	273/318/340 360	front	left	550	20½	25	31	29½	28	29½	23½
MoPar V8	383/400/440	front	left	670	23½	29½	30½	30	28	29	24
MoPar Hemi	426	center	left	690	28½	29	31	31	28	32	24
Olds V8	330/350/455	rear	left	600	21½	26½	31	31	27	29	24
Pontiac V8	350/400	rear	left	590	22	27	31	29	26	28½	27
Pontiac V8	455	rear	right	640	23	27	33	32	28½	29½	27
Cadillac V8	472/500	middle	right	600	23½	28	32	30½	29	30	28½

ENGINE SPECIFICATION CHART — A lot of guesswork will be saved by consulting this chart. It shows all important dimensions you need for determining "if it will fit." The letters A through G refer to the dimensions shown in the drawings on page 22.

(Left) Sure it will fit—but what about the air cleaner? More than one engine swap forces cutting a hole in the hood . . . which in turn means fabricating a scoop to hide the air cleaner. Maybe you're willing to live with this . . . and maybe you aren't.

Bailing wire is very effective in holding an engine in the correct location when it is being leveled and mounts are fabricated.

WHAT GETS SWAPPED?

Somewhere along the way—while you are measuring engines, under hood clearances and finding out what is available in the way of stock and aftermarket hardware you must determine exactly what gets swapped. Determining which components to swap must be predicated on the swap itself and why it is being done in the first place. If you are installing a small block Ford and automatic transmission in a Ford Pinto because you already have the necessary components and plan to drive the car back and forth to work, you can probably get by without changing the rear axle assembly. If you are doing the swap because you want a fun car to drive and plan to drive it with some vigor, then the rear axle should be changed. Obviously if the swap is being done for an all-out competi-

tion machine, a larger axle set up especially for racing **must** be installed.

Full size V8 engines normally require full size axle assemblies in order to provide reliability. There are always exceptions. I know of a small block Chevy and Powerglide installed in a Vega. The stock axle was retained. The car is driven by a young housewife—and is never driven hard. The husband who did the swap never drives the car. He admitted to us and to himself that even with the Powerglide transmission he would stick his foot far enough into the throttle frequently enough to fail the rear axle.

If you are contemplating installing a full size engine in a compact car, then you should flip over to our chapter or rear axle swapping. Here again, before actually getting into the swap you should determine what is practical for you.

Hardware You Can Buy

Decide, as best you can, how your swap will be done. By this we mean, don't yank the existing engine out, buy another engine, block it into place and start fabricating mounts until you have given some thought to the scope of the swap. Although this may seem like covering old ground, we are trying to do everything possible to make your swap go easily.

EXPLORE STOCK HARDWARE

Stock hardware is low cost, reliable and readily available. These are all solid reasons why you should know as much about what is available as possible. As we have pointed out before, there are subtle differences in hardware. Earlier we gave the example of there being different oil pans for the same engine—the same goes for intake manifolds, water pumps and exhaust manifolds. Not all engines will have a long and short shaft water pump, though, and the way you find out is to keep right on looking at engines and talking to parts men. If you are pretty sure the left side exhaust manifold will interfere with the steering box, then you should make every effort to locate different stock exhaust manifolds for your engine before

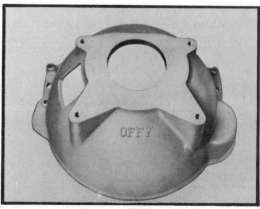

One of the more popular pieces of hardware manufactured by Trans-Dapt is this adapter which mates any small block Chevy to a Jeep transmission.

This Offenhauser adapter mates all small block and large block Chevy engines to all three and four speed Ford transmissions built since 1965.

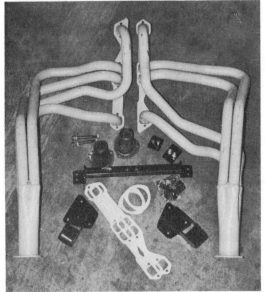

(Above) Advance Adapters and Novak build hardware which allows mating one of several automatic transmissions with a variety of four wheel drive transfer cases.

(Above) Some of the Advance Adapter kits even include headers to be used in conjunction with their motor mounts.

(Right) This is the small block Chevy to Toyota transmission and transfer case package made possible by Advance.

giving up on the swap or convincing yourself that special headers are the only way out of the problem.

EXPLORE NON-STOCK HARDWARE

The manufacturing and selling of engine swap hardware in the United States is a large and growing business. Engine mounts, transmission mounts, adapters and special exhaust systems for specific swaps are available. On the following pages we will outline what is available, listing sources by name and a few descriptive words. Knowing that mounts are available for a certain swap can save immense amounts of time.

Advance Adapters Inc.
1645 Commerce Way
Paso Robles, CA 93446
Phone (805) 238-7000
Catalog $1.00

This firm is the leading manufacturer of four

Hurst kits come in various stages. Their conversion aids have helped engine swappers for twenty years.

Hurst pioneered the use of the Ford type rubber doughnut mount which is quite adaptable and easy for the amateur to use.

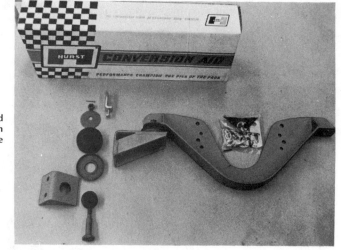

wheel drive adapter hardware. They have a very complete line of transmission-to-transfer case adapter hardware. If you decide you want a small block Ford in your Jeep, Advance can supply you with the hardware needed to mate the rear of the Ford C4 automatic transmission with the front of the Jeep transfer case. They also have a good selection of engine mounts and engine-to-trans - mission adapters that are related to off-road type swaps. The Advance catalog also lists header systems designed specifically for vehicles that have undergone an engine transplant. A Chevy in a Toyota and a Chevy in a Jeep are just two examples.

Ansen Enterprises Inc.
8924 Bellanca Ave.
Los Angeles, CA 90045
Phone (213) 670-7860
Catalog $1.00

Ansen manufactures a diverse line of high performance equipment. A considerable number of the items are designed just for the engine swapper. Ansen has a complete line of safety housings which fit between the engine and transmission and are required in most forms of racing. These safety housings are designed so a Chevy engine can be used with a Ford transmission, etc. Frame adapters, motor mounts and rear crossmembers are also part of the Ansen line. They have double and single swing pedals which mount to the firewall and can be used to solve the problem of installing clutch linkage.

Sway-A-Way Suspension Components
7840 Burnett Avenue
Van Nuys, CA 91405
(818) 988-5510

These folks have a transmission mounting kit designed to mount a VW transmission into any type of frame. They also manufacture torsion bars, sway bar kits and other specialized suspension components for VW, Porsche and mini trucks. If you need beefed up suspension after swapping a bigger engine in your VW or mini truck, be sure to check Sway-A-Way's catalog.

Crown Manufacturing Co., Inc.
137 W. 157th
Gardena, CA 90248
(213) 327-7670
Catalog $2.00

Crown got into the swapping business by designing and manufacturing hardware needed to install Corvair engines in VWs. Now they have all the hardware necessary to install small and large block Chevys in the back seat area of Corvairs. The resulting Corveights are pure delight to those who like to give others a surprise—which a Corveight is guaranteed to do! The Corveight kit is very complete in that it attends to needed suspension changes when the V-8 is added. If you are into Corvairs or VWs, you need the Crown catalog.

Mid Engineering
P.O. Box 14007
Lansing, MI 48901
Phone (517) 323-7610
Catalog $5.00

These folks are specialists in mid-engined chassis and conversion components. Some of their packages include the Toronado automatic GT frame kit, V6 and V8 Corvair four-speed GT frame kit, Toronado mid-T roadster package, a universal mid-engine modular subframe (this replaces a unibody frame section and adapts an engine mounting to a mid-engine configuration), a mid-engine Toronado/Corvair conversion package for the Corvair body, a Buick V6 conversion package for the Corvair, and a Chevy V8-to-Toronado

conversion package. Their GT frame kits are designed to be used with the GT kit cars such as the Kelmark, Manta, Aztec, Sterling, etc., to replace the VW 94-inch wheelbase unibody and engine/transaxle.

Wilcap
2930 Sepulveda Blvd.
Torrance, CA 90503
(213) 326-9200

These folks have a small line of engine to transmission adaptors for domestic engines. They also have some flywheels. They've been in business for about 25 years.

Trans-Dapt of California, Inc.
16410 Manning Way
Cerritos, CA 90701
Phone (213) 404-2985
Catalog $3.00

Trans-Dapt has been a Godsend to a couple of generations of enthusiasts with bellhousing-type transmission adapters and engine-to-transmission adapter plates allowing the use of the existing engine bellhousing. They carry pilot bushings and some engine mounts. Trans-Dapt also manufactures a complete line of oil filter bypass and

Hurst even manufactures an "engine grabber" which bolts the intake manifold and facilitates removing and replacing engines.

Several firms manufacture the hardware which allows for the remote placement of the oil filter. In this application the filter would have hit a crossmember.

block-off adapters and remote oil filter brackets. They might not be able to solve all of your swap problems, but the items they list can solve a lot of them.

Don Hardy Race Cars
202 West Missouri St.
Floydada, Texas 79235
Phone (806) 983-3774

Don has conversion kits for large and small block Chevy engines being placed into Vegas— primarily for drag racing. A recent addition to his excellent line of hardware is the small block Chevy into LUV pickup kit.

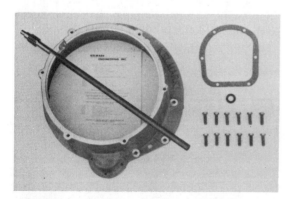

Mid Engineering sells the hardware necessary to bolt any Chevy V8 to a Corvair transaxle.

Quickor Engineering
6710 SW 111th St.
Beaverton, OR 97005
Phone (503) 646-8600

Quickor features heavy duty suspension packages and separate components for many brands and models of cars. Write for their complete catalog.

Kennedy Engineered Products (KEP)
10202 Glenoaks Blvd.
Pacoima, CA 91331
Phone (818) 899-2612
Catalog No Charge

KEP specializes in adapters and all related hardware needed when installing a variety of small engines in vehicles equipped with a VW, Porsche, Pantera, Corvair or Subaru transaxle. The list of engines that can be bolted to these is a long one— Colt, Mazda, Pinto, Volvo, Vega, Ford and GM V8s and V6s, Capri V6 and Alfa Romeo. Kennedy has been in business since the late 1960s. Much of his hardware winds up in dune buggies and in hot street driven vehicles.

Rancho Suspension
6925 Atlantic Avenue
Long Beach, CA 90805
(213) 423-0477

Rancho has a series of specially engineered road performance suspension systems for many different domestic cars. After you complete your swap and realize that you need to improve the suspension, get a catalog from Rancho and check out what they offer.

Neal Products Inc.
7170 Ronson Road
San Diego, CA 92111
(619) 565-9336

Got a problem where the swap works, but the linkages don't? Try Neal Products. They have hydraulic throttle and clutch assemblies, and gas, brake and clutch pedal assemblies. You can probably find something that will work after reading their catalog.

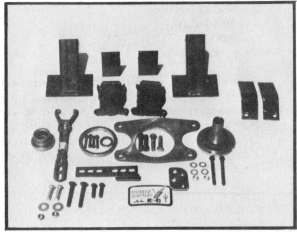

Advance builds this very complete kit to ease the installation of Chevy V8 into Toyota Landcruiser.

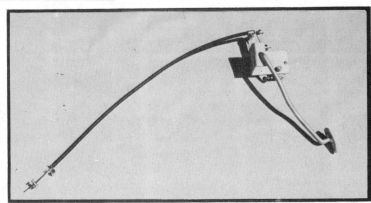

This is the universal type cable throttle unit marketed by Advance. This will work out quite well in most any installation.

Rod Simpson Hybrids
P.O. Box 25779
Los Angeles, CA 90025
(213) 826-3304

These guys can slide a Chevy small block V8 right into a Porsche 911 or 914 for you. Or, into a Datsun, if you want.

Nobu's Auto Lab Inc.
6366 DeLongpre Avenue
Hollywood, CA 90028
(213) 462-2018

This firm is a specialist in swapping a Chevy small block V8 into the Datsun Z car.

Hurst Performance, Inc.
50 West Street Road
Warminster, PA 18974
Phone (215) 672-5000
Catalog $1.00

George Hurst was not the first man to do an engine swap or even the first to market hardware to aid in swapping, but George Hurst deserves credit as the man who built a company and then led an entire industry into engine swapping. Today, Hurst is into suspension components and drive gear items such as clutches and gears in addition to their now-famous line of shifters for stick and automatic transmissions. But Hurst is still in the business of turning out a huge line of frame mounts, motor mounts, cross members, dropped drag links, and electrical conversion kits. Their conversion system components are related to all popular domestic engines and vehicles.

Novak Enterprises, Inc.
13321 Alondra
Santa Fe Springs, CA 90670
Phone (213) 921-3202
Catalog $2.00

Novak specializes in mounts and adapters for installing various engines in off-road vehicles. His specialty is in dealing with Jeep-built vehicles. His conversion hardware does not end with changing an engine and transmission in a vehicle; hardware is available which allows upgrading the steering and brakes. This is a small manufacturer with an excellent reputation.

Speedway Motors
300 Van Dorn
P.O. Box 81906
Lincoln, NE 68501
(402) 474-4411

Speedway has frame mounts and brackets for mounting many different engines in a variety of applications. In fact, if you're going to be doing any engine swapping, Speedway Motors' huge catalog is a must!

Lett's Build-A-Rod
11601 McKinley
Houston, TX 77038
713) 447-5388

They have custom-machined T-6 aluminum motor mounts for small and big block Chevys. Come with universal weld-on tabs. Also mounts for GM TH350 and TH400 transmissions, with urethane mounting bushings. They will also custom build trans mounts for Ford and Chrysler transmissions.

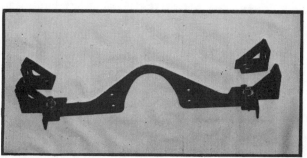

Hurst, Ansen and Advance handle these yoke type mounts to mate most late V8 engines to earlier frames.

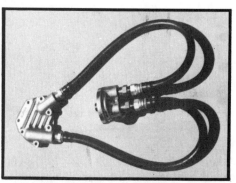

This is just one of the many adapters available which facilitate the job of remotely locating the oil filter.

Hooker
1008 W. Brooks
Ontario, CA 91762
Phone (714) 983-5871

Hooker has engine mount and headers for small block Chevy and Buick V6 engines into most mini-pickups. They also have a large and small block Chevy swap kit for the Vega.

Offenhauser Sales Corporation
5300 Alhambra Ave.
Los Angeles, CA 90032
Phone (213) 225-1307

The Offenhauser reputation is solid and the company is primarily known today for their full line of intake manifolds for domestic and foreign engines. However the company has a full line of engine-to-transmission adapters, oil filter bypass and block-off plates for two and four wheel drive vehicles stretching back to the days of the flat-head Ford. They also carry carburetor leveling blocks primarily intended for marine installations —but useful in some engine swaps.

Borg Warner Corporation
Automotive Parts Division
11045 Gage Ave.
Franklin Park, Illinois 60131

Spicer Division
Dana Corporation
P. O. Box 321
Toledo, Ohio 43691

TRW
Replacement Division
8001 E. Pleasant Valley Road
Cleveland, Ohio 44131
Phone (216) 383-0121

None of the above companies are into manufacturing hardware specifically designed to be used in engine swaps. All manufacture and distribute OEM and replacement driveline components. Their catalogs not only list applications but give line drawings with dimensions on yokes, shafts and companion flanges of all sizes and shapes. Some of this information can be extremely valuable in some swap problems.

Advance sells all the hardware you need to adapt a Muncie four speed transmission to a Jeep or Scout transfer case—which is a pretty good idea if you plan to go to small block Chevy power.

With the Hoosier adapter shown here, a Ford four speed, all-synchro "top loader" transmission can be adapted to a Scout transfer case. Hoosier has a full line of similar adapters.

Buying An Engine

Buying an engine for your swap should be carried out exactly like your approach to the swap itself. You must consider what is practical for you. Cash, time and skill all must be considered if you are to make a wise judgment in what you finally buy. Take your time and think it through—then do a lot of shopping. We can divide engines for swaps into three general categories—new, used and rebuilt or remanufactured. There are drawbacks and advantages to buying an engine in any category. Do not overlook that—but most importantly, do not overlook the simple fact you must determine what is practical for you in your situation. First, let's take a look at new engines.

NEW ENGINES

The advantage of a new engine is that it is new. It is assembled by the factory that builds thousands—if not hundreds of thousands of engines just like it every year. Although I will get some argument on this, most domestic engines will give 100,000 miles of service before needing a rebuild. Obviously, if you neglect the engine or burn rubber in every gear at every light, the 100,000-mile figure goes out the door. New engines can be

bought in two ways—complete, or in pieces. In either case, you go to the dealership to get the engine. Although you want a complete engine, you will not get one. Something will be missing . . . and the something will vary from one make to another. On one it may be the emission control equipment and starter—on another it may be the alternator and carburetor. It varies. To make the engine run, you will have to come up with the missing parts, either from a parts counter or a wrecking yard. Buying a complete engine at a dealership and then adding on the parts needed to make it run can be expensive. It may be reliable and new, but it will be expensive.

There is another way to buy a new engine—in parts. Don't laugh. This is done by a select group of individiuals and you should know about it. What this entails is going to the dealer and ordering every major component it takes to build a particular engine and then assembling all of the parts. In most cases, the new parts are laced with some used ones—why buy a new starter, alternator, intake manifold or oil pan if a used one is up to the task? The aficianados who follow this route take pains to balance the moving parts, double check all clearances upon assembly and

When buying an engine in a wrecking yard, select one in a car if at all possible. You can get a pretty fair idea of why the car is there, mileage and the general condition of the vehicle before it wound up hanging off the back of a tow truck.

generally spend a lot of time in putting everything together. If they are talented and patient, the engine can run like a fine watch—and give them performance unavailable with a factory-assembled engine. If they are not up to the task of gathering all of the necessary parts and carrying through with the time-consuming task of putting it all together they are likely to wind up with an engine far worse than what they can buy assembled at the dealership or they wind up with an engine that will not start. The advantages of this approach lie along the lines of a smoother running, higher performance engine capable of increased life. By the substitution of non-stock parts, the engine may be finely tuned in a particular direction to suit the swapper.

The disadvantages lie along the lines of increased cost and time to build the complete engine and the amount of skill needed to complete the job.

If you are thorough about your quest in learning the ins and outs of swapping economics, then you will not pass over new engines lightly. Visit the local dealership handling the brand of engine you need. Tell them specifically what you have in mind. Ask what the engine costs, and exactly what you get for that amount of money. When they are talking about a complete engine you want to know if that includes the essential items of carburetor, intake manifold, distributor, wiring, starter, alternator, water pump, and fan. Ask a lot of questions. Write down the answers.

USED ENGINES

By far the most popular choice for the majority

I would consider this a bad buy, unless the cost of the engine was roughly the value of the engine as scrap iron. Obviously the engine was not cared for in addition to the fact that there are now some major and expensive components missing.

of engine swappers is the used engine. On any given day there are literally tens of thousands of used engines available for sale in the United States. Most wrecking yards are linked by a tele-type system and they will cooperate in finding you the engine you want. Cost and availability are big advantages of buying a used engine. The disad-vantage, of course, is that you are buying an unknown quality. You know the engine is used, but you don't know how used. If at all possible, select an engine still in a wrecked car. The condi-tion of the car can often tell you a lot about the condition of the engine. If the vehicle appears to have been well maintained up until the time it was wrecked, the engine was probably cared for in a like manner. If at all possible, have the wrecking yard personnel fire the engine up for you. This can be done—even if the engine has been removed

Ah, how sweet it is—a new engine straight from a dealer. Note, however, that the engine is not complete—and those pieces will drive the cost of the engine ever upward.

An engine in this condition can be fired in the yard—unfortunately, the open exhaust will muffle expensive internal engine noises. About all you can do is check the oil, a couple of spark plugs and the general outward appearance to determine mileage and condition.

from the car. If you can convince the wrecking yard you are serious about buying an engine they can start it for you. For a small fee, most yards will even deliver an engine for you if you live within the area. Most yards will even guarantee the major parts of an engine to be mechanically sound for a given period of time—usually 60 or 90 days. However, you should get this in writing on the bill of sale. Many yards will supply you with another engine instead of returning your money if the first engine turns out to be a sick turkey. Do some shopping—for engines, prices, conditions and guarantees. There are a lot of engines around so take your time. There are several common sense areas of thought to be followed when buying a used engine in addition to what we have already

pointed out. Stay away from an engine that has been through a fire. Check an engine carefully for physical damage. If an oil pan was ripped open in a long skid, the engine could have run out of oil while still running and at the same time ingested some dirt and gravel. Bad news. The oil filter should also be intact for the same reason. A damaged crank pulley or dampner could mean the crank received a severe blow in the front and this could cause expensive internal damages. The same thing goes for the tailshaft of the trans-mission. If a car has suffered a crippling blow from the rear, the axle can move forward and shove the driveshaft far enough into the transmission to break something, so watch for this when buying an engine and transmission together.

Take a long hard look before laying out cash for a wrecking yard engine. Normally, there are more engines than buyers.

Oddly enough, the most common mistake an amateur engine swapper can make when buying an engine is to not buy everything needed. Buy guts, feathers, claw, linkage, brackets, wiring, starter, alternator and so on. Unless you have a private wrecking yard supply of parts in your garage so you can fill in the missing pieces, buying them—new or used—will drive the cost of the engine ever upward in addition to costing you a lot of time.

REBUILT AND REMANUFACTURED

Rebuilt and remanufactured engines are available through engine rebuilding firms, parts houses and garages. Rebuilt engines generally have been fitted with new rings and bearings—and if the cylinder heads are included—a valve job. Other components are replaced or rebuilt if they are needed. A manufactured engine generally means more components get more attention and more get replaced. Naturally, this is reflected in the cost. For the swapper, these engines are rarely a good buy since they are not complete engines. They are sold as short blocks and long blocks. Generally, the long block version includes the heads, intake manifold and water pump while the short block does not. This saves you money since you simply bolt on the components you already have. But in the case of engine swapping, you most likely will not have the missing components so you are faced with the prospect of rounding up a lot of hardware at parts counters and wrecking yards. This costs money and time.

I consider buying an engine from an individual

This engine is straight out of a wreck—but what a wreck—a pickup with less than 5,000 miles on it got hit from the side. This turned out to be an excellent buy.

a very risky situation. Maybe the engine he is trying to sell is stolen or maybe the engine is for sale because it is no good. Take your time—do a lot of shopping. There are far more engines out there than there are guys wanting to swap them.

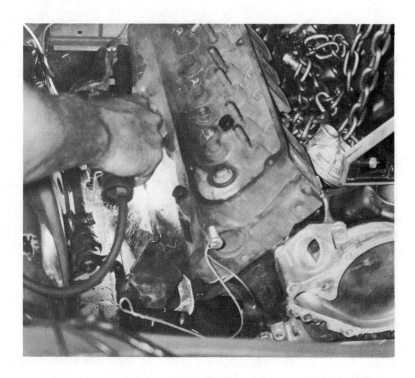

Engine Mounts

There are two basic areas of concern with motor mounts when doing an engine swap—where they should go, and how they should be constructed. The question of where they should go is solved immediately if you are adapting a new engine to the existing transmission. Once the engine is lowered into place and bolted to the transmission, the engine should be lowered as far as practical, leveled, held in place and mounts constructed or bolted into place if aftermarket items are being used. Although in a situation like this you have no control over the fore and aft location of the engine, you normally have some control over how low the engine sits in the chassis. Spend some time at this and get it right. With the weight of the engine on the chassis, you should determine if the carburetor mounting flange on the intake manifold is reasonably level fore and aft and laterally. Exhaust manifold clearance with the frame or steering gear should also be considered. By raising the engine ½-inch and spacing the transmission upward ¼-inch at the rear, it might be possible to keep the engine level and at the same time provide clearance between the exhaust manifold and steering box. Although this might not be the very best placement for the engine from an engi-

neering standpoint, it might be the most practical solution to the problem for you. If you stop thinking, and start welding at this point, you are bound to have trouble with the swap. Haste makes for very expensive waste in engine swapping. Vibration is an all too common problem in swapping and it can often be traced directly to improper driveline phasing.

DRIVELINE PHASING

Driveline phasing—proper or improper—is difficult, if not impossible, to photograph—and in some respects very difficult to explain. That doesn't make it any less important for a successful swap.

Improper driveline phasing comes about this way. You lower the new engine and transmission into the car, jiggle it around like we've suggested so the exhaust manifold doesn't interfere with the steering box and you shove the engine forward just enough to be able to remove the valve cover without it scraping the firewall. You make sure the carb mounting plate on the intake manifold is reasonably level and there is sufficient clearance between the crank pulley and the crossmember so

This is a flame cutter which is what a professional engine swapper uses to fabricate mounts. The cutter follows a template and transfers the design to the steel plate. Most large metal working shops have a cutter like this.

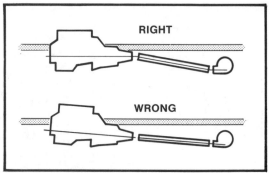

The axis of the pinion gear should be parallel with the center line of the transmission tailshaft. In other words, the universal joints are supposed to work—not just act as an extension of the driveshaft.

Scoot under the car and hold the protractor base flush against the nose of the pinion gear shaft or rotate the pinion flange until it is vertical and lay the protractor base against it. Rotate the protractor head until the bubble indicates level. Now, using the little locking screw on the protractor head, lock the head in place on the protractor. You can now read the position of the pinion gear axis relative to the ground. Let's say it

the fan belt can be replaced. At this point we can safely say this is roughly how most engine swaps proceed—and at this point most engine swappers will fabricate the necessary mounts or weld in the mounts they have bought. The results of an engine swap performed by the method described above can be nice in appearance but one plagued with strange sounds and vibrations. This is because the driveline was not phased.

Imagine a complete automotive drivetrain from the side—engine, transmission, driveshaft and rear axle assembly. To properly phase the driveline, the tailshaft of the transmission must be parallel with the axis of the pinion gear. Let's say the axis of the pinion gear is parallel with the ground. This means the tailshaft of the transmission must also be parallel to the ground. This may be good information, but how do you figure all of this out laying upside down under a car with an engine propped into place with a bunch of two-by-fours and an old floor jack? Actually, the process is pretty simple. All you need is a protractor with a built-in level. This is about a fifteen dollar item available in the tool department of most hardware stores.

There are a lot of protractor type tools around— but the one you want for this job is one with a reversible head and a built-in level. If you can find one with a magnetic base, buy it.

With a steady hand a regular cutting torch can be used to shape the parts needed for a mount. Note that both hands rest on the metal to steady the torch.

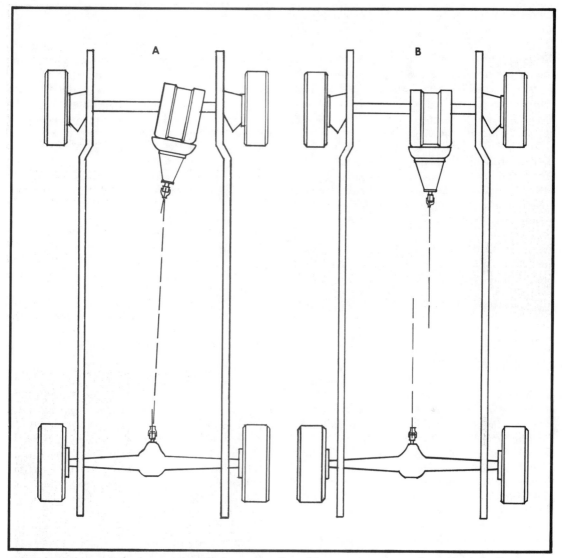

Drawing A represents the wrong way to offset an engine. Done this way, you are sure to have driveshaft vibration, noise and U-joint wear. Drawing B shows the correct method of offsetting the engine.

was 80 degrees. That means the pinion gear axis is tilted slightly upward at the nose. Now slide forward under the car and attach the protractor to the tailshaft of the transmission. Follow the same procedure of getting the bubble level and take a reading. Let's say it is 90 degrees. If the engine is left in this position and the rear axle assembly is not moved, the driveline will be out of phase since 90 degrees plus 80 degrees is 170 degrees. To be in phase, the tailshaft and the pinion gear must be parallel. To achieve that, the sum of the two angles—that of the transmission tailshaft and the nose on the pinion gear—must be 180 degrees. At this point you can look over the situation and decide whether to point the tailshaft down a little or rotate the axle slightly so the axis of the pinion gear is level with the world.

If you are switching axle assemblies at the same time you are swapping engines and have not welded the spring perches onto the axle tubes, then rotating the axle and changing the angle of the pinion is the simple way out of the problem. If you plan to retain the axle, then a wedge shim can be placed between the spring perch and the spring pack. These shims are easy to come by; they come in a variety of sizes and wedges of different degrees, and are used by shops specializing in frame alignment.

If there are no clearance problems in the engine room, you can raise the nose of the engine enough to put the tailshaft at the correct angle. Just move the engine a little, and re-measure. Keep moving and measuring until the two angles add up to 180 degrees. OK, let's say you decided to leave the axle alone and have jiggled the engine around so the protractor reading on the tailshaft reads 100 degrees. That plus the 80 degrees in the rear end gives you the desired 180 degrees. Fine. This means the driveline is phased in a vertical plane—but not necessarily in the horizontal plane.

Now, imagine looking straight down at the drivetrain from the rafters of your garage. The pinion gear axis will be perpendicular to the crossmembers in the car—assuming of course the axle is installed correctly in the chassis and that the frame is square. We could also say the pinion gear is parallel with the frame rails, but this gets to be confusing at times because most frame rails are now curved. Because we would throw the entire chassis out of alignment if we twisted the axle (horizontally) in the frame, we can only move the engine and transmission in order to achieve correct horizontal driveline phasing. Once again the object is to get the tailshaft of the transmission parallel with the pinion gear. This requires more measuring and maybe more jiggling. Let's say that when you first lowered the engine into the frame that the exhaust manifold touched the steering box. You moved the engine over so there was ½-inch of clearance between the manifold and the box. There's nothing wrong with this—as long as the front of the engine is moved over the exact amount the transmission tailshaft is moved over. Starting at the very center of the crankshaft dampner, measure to both sides of the frame. Let's say that from the crank center to the frame on the right is 13 inches. From crank center to the frame on the left is 15½ inches. Hmmmm . . . you jiggled

it a little more than you thought. No big deal. Slide under the car and measure from the center of the transmission output shaft to the frame rails again. Unless the frame rails are parallel all the way back, you won't come up with that 15½ and 13-inch measurement again no matter how the engine is set in the frame. The difference in the two measurements front to rear is what counts. If the left side frame to tailshaft measures 18-inches, then the right side should be 15½-inches to produce the same difference there was at the front of the engine. This will place the engine straight in the chassis—but off-set. That's OK. The driveshaft will now be properly phased and the tailshaft will be aligned horizontally and vertically with the axis of the pinion gear. Wire or support everything so it doesn't move. At this point you can begin to construct or install the mounts.

If you've purchased a set of aftermarket mounts and feel you have no choice in where the engine is placed in the chassis, you are only partially correct. You will not have the wide latitude of adjustment offered by constructing your own mounts, but in most cases you don't need a lot of latitude. Regardless of the type mounts you are using, the previously explained method of checking driveline phasing should be used. Before the mounts are attached to the frame, you have some latitude as to where they will be placed. You may have to space the transmission mount up or down a little or slot a mounting hole a little to get it all aligned—but do it. If you go to all of the trouble to do an engine swap, phase the driveline.

Obviously, the driveline phasing procedure just described applies only to an open driveshaft arrangement. If a torque tube driveline is involved, the axis of the crankshaft should pass straight through the transmission mainshaft and into the driveshaft and pinion gear. Only in a torque tube arrangement should this be a straight line and it

This is the type of protractor (properly called an inclinometer) you should use.

should be straight when the weight of the engine is on the frame and the car is carrying a normal load. Naturally, there will be some variance between theory and practice since the rear end will move up and down on the road and the loading of the car will vary from day to day.

In a torque tube driveline, it is important that the tube have a slight downward angle from the rear of the transmission to the rear axle. This prevents lubricant in the rear axle from running into the torque tube and loading the universal joint at the forward end.

THREE POINT VERSUS FOUR POINT MOUNTING

A long time ago automotive engineers figured out that the engine and transmission unit in a passenger car needed to be held in the chassis at three points—not two, not four—but three. This allows the engine and transmission to flex the proper amount in the chassis as torque loads rise and fall. This also keeps the power train from transmitting an excessive amount of noise and vibration into the chassis. Noise and vibration are of secondary importance in a truck and because of the high stresses imposed on mount hardware

by high torque engines most large trucks and many light duty trucks use a four point mounting system.

In figure 4 we show four correct ways of mounting an engine in a passenger car—A thru D. The four-point mounting system used in trucks is shown in Figure 4 E. Figure 4 A shows the most common stock method of mounting a V8 in a modern chassis. Six and four cylinder engines of the past ten years or so have also been mounted this way. A single mount is placed near the area of the transmission with the load at this point bearing directly on a crossmember. At the engine, a mount is placed on either side of the block with the junction point being the inside of the frame rails—or in some cases a crossmember that passes between the frame rails. In Detroit, mounting points are located by computer analysis to minimize noise and vibration. For this reason, I would suggest using stock mounting locations on the block whenever possible.

The example given in 4 B was used in the early days of the Chevy V8 and continues to be a popular solution to the mount problem when 4 A isn't practical. A single mount is again used at the rear of the transmission, but the two mounts on

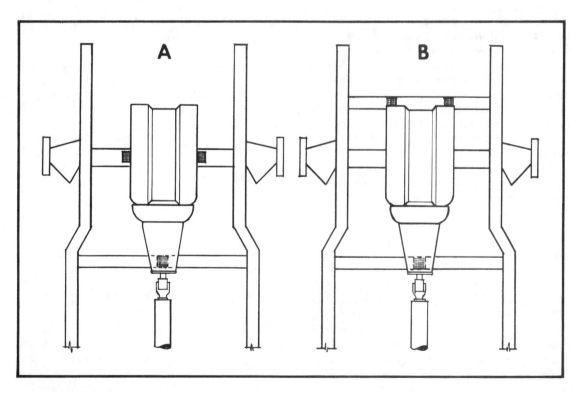

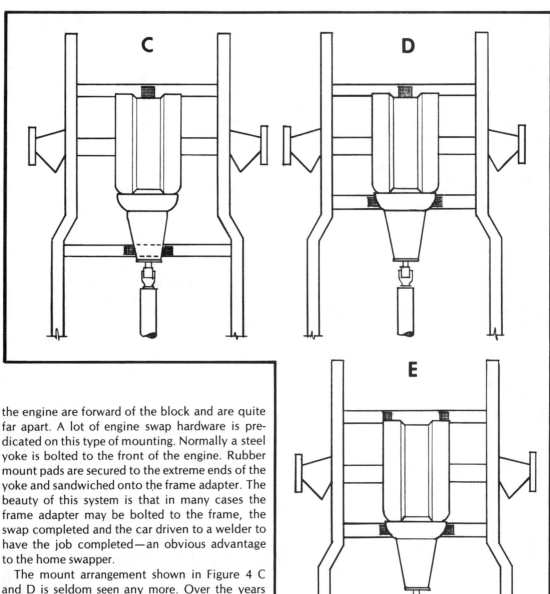

C D E

the engine are forward of the block and are quite far apart. A lot of engine swap hardware is predicated on this type of mounting. Normally a steel yoke is bolted to the front of the engine. Rubber mount pads are secured to the extreme ends of the yoke and sandwiched onto the frame adapter. The beauty of this system is that in many cases the frame adapter may be bolted to the frame, the swap completed and the car driven to a welder to have the job completed—an obvious advantage to the home swapper.

The mount arrangement shown in Figure 4 C and D is seldom seen any more. Over the years many six cylinder engines and some V8 engines utilized a single point mounting in the front of the block and two mounting points in the area of the bellhousing or at the rear of the transmission. In most swaps, either of these methods can be used, but normally they are just plain inconvenient. In the vast majority of cases, there is simply nothing to be gained by mounting the power train in this manner. For best engineering, a crossmember must be directly under the front mount—and that is often inconvenient. In the example of D, the rear mounting could obviously pose an interference problem for clutch linkage, steering box and exhaust pipes—it all depends on the swap.

The four point mounting shown in 4 E should be reserved for mounting engines—either a six or an eight—in a truck. This mounts the engine more rigidly and will eliminate some of the flex found in a three point mounting. This, in turn, increases noise and torsional vibration. Save this method of mounting for trucks only.

FABRICATING MOUNTS

Normally, the second question of swapping is along the lines of: "Are there mounts available for this swap?" What this means is—does anyone make the mounts so I can buy them and bolt them in, because I have no idea where to start. Because making engine mounts (not "motor mounts!") takes a small amount of thinking, there is a tendancy to panic before the problem is analyzed. The problem is rather simple—how to attach the engine to the chassis in a workmanlike manner to prevent it from moving about. That's it.

In the first place, you should know there are mounts readily available for most of the popular engine swaps. Our suppliers list contains the information necessary to establish contact with most of the manufacturers of engine swap hardware—including engine mounts. There is nothing "magic" about store-bought mounts just as there is no "magic" to what it takes to make your own—or have them made.

Let us assume—for the sake of relieving your mind—that we are installing a Belchfire Eight into a 1955 Zot (very rare). No store-bought mounts are available. How do you proceed to solve the

problem given the following parameters?

1. You do not weld or know how to use a cutting torch.
2. You live in East Overshoe, South Dakota where no one has **ever** done an engine swap before.
3. You can begin the swap on Friday afternoon and must be able to drive the swapped Zot to work Monday morning.

Given these parameters what do you do first? Forget it. As long as we are dealing with numbers one and two we can help, but when you throw in number three we have to point back to the word "practical" in the title of this book—and remind you that number three on our list here is simply not practical. So let's stick with what is practical and proceed.

The first step is to correctly locate the engine in the chassis. We've already been through that—so a major part of the battle is over.

The entire mount "unit" can be broken down into two or sometimes three parts on all mounts we've ever seen in a car or light truck. The two-part mount unit consists of a rubber and steel

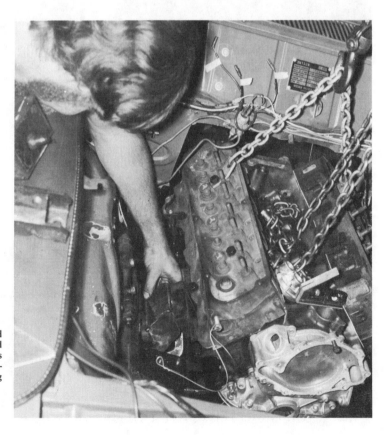

After a mount is tack welded together, it should be installed and checked for fit before the welding is completed. This goes for any fabrication in an engine swap requiring welding.

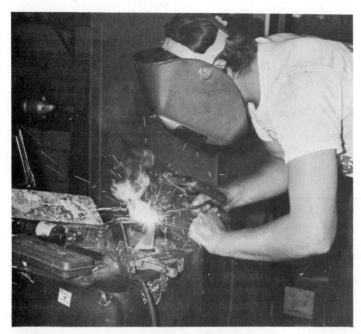

Fabricated mounts should be arc welded or heli-arced together. Any welding shop can handle a job like this.

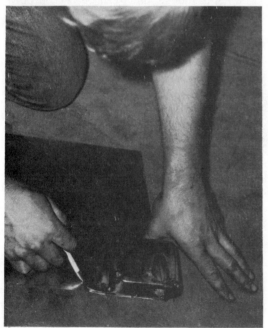

(Above) After both mounts are tacked together, they should both be bolted in place before final welding. At this point you should determine if the mounts interfere with exhaust manifolds, fuel pump, etc. A little work now prevents a lot of work later on.

(Above) If the mounts are to be the same on both sides, a mount tacked together can be used as a template for the remaining side. In the beginning stages of making mounts, light cardboard or sheet metal is the ideal choice for template material.

(Right) After all welding has been completed, the mount can be painted and bolted in position to properly locate the engine while the rest of the work continues. Note that the original frame mount is left in place for the time being—a good idea.

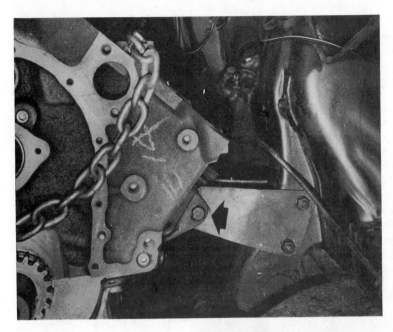

A sandwich-type mount works out well on vehicles having unitized construction. A spacer of some type must be used between the two plates (arrow) to keep the engine side of the mount from collapsing inward.

Frame mounts may be attached to crossmembers as well as frames. This can certainly solve clearance problems with exhaust manifolds and steering box.

bonded unit that bolts to the engine. This is one part—and in all cases it is a part which can be unbolted, thrown away and replaced. The second part is properly called a frame mount. It attaches to the frame or a crossmember with bolts, rivets or welding. In the case of a car without a frame - Pinto, Vega, etc., the frame mount is an integral part of the subframe stamping.

In the three-part mount, the rubber is not bonded to the engine mount. In this case there is a metal tab which bolts to the block, the rubber insulator, and the frame mount. Not much difference is there? In an engine swap the engine side of engine mounts can bolt to the block in the same location of the stock mounts or they can be fashioned to mount in an other-than-stock location. To minimize noise and vibration and to make one engine readily adaptable to any number of vehicles within the line, a manufacturer will spend a considerable amount of effort to determine the very best location for an engine mount. In the vast majority of engine swaps, this is the mount location that should be used. However, you should know there are thousands of successful engine swaps on the streets today which were accomplished with mounts bolted to a non-stock location on the block.

In using a factory mounting location on the block, you can take advantage of factory engineering to reduced noise and vibration. Stock rubber-bonded mounts can be used to join the gap between frame and block. Although we favor this method of mounting, there can be disadvantages in some swaps. Depending on the chassis/engine combination the stock location on the block can make it almost impossible to use a stock mount and a fabricated frame mount. When extensive fabrication and modification to the frame is involved, it is far more practical for most individuals to go to a non-stock engine mount location. Normally, this means going to a three piece mount.

The two and three piece mounts we've described are used in 99% of all swaps. There is one other category and we don't recommend this except for all-out competition (and then it is controversial). We're speaking of the solid mount. No rubber is involved—and every bit of vibration and noise from the engine is transmitted into the chassis, subframe or body. There are valid reasons for using this type of mount on an all-out competition car, but no reasons for using solid mounting for a car driven on the streets.

Now that we are back to east Overshoe, South Dakota with our engine swap, we will proceed on

This is the Herbert mount to install a small block Chevy in a Vega. Note the frame mount bolts to the stock Vega mount location and then runs forward to pick up the stock mounting location on the block.

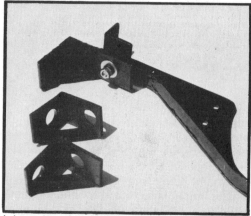

This is a universal type yoke mount which allows a small block Chevy to be bolted into most anything. Note that the holes are offset in the frame mounting taps to accomodate different width frames.

The end view of the forward running crossmember mount reveals 3/16-inch plate boxed at the crossmember and stock rubber mount—a workmanlike simple approach to a problem.

Here's a universal yoke mount installed on a small block Chevy. Note the rubber biscuit between the yoke and the frame mount and note how the frame mount is braced from the underside.

In some installations, engine mounting can be facilitated by building a crossmember to fit between the frame rails and pass under the engine and attach to the stock mounts.

Heavy, flat plate used for the engine mount is popular with some segments of engine swappers. Because the strength of the mount is almost solely dependant on the thickness of the metal, 3/8-inch thick must be used — even with small block engines to insure the mount does not fail.

This is the crossmember mount in a '51 Ford pickup. The mount supports a small block Chevy.

Heavy wall square tubing, such as 2" x 2", .095" wall, is readily available and easy to work with in many mounting situations. The flat plate at the end of the tubing gets welded to the frame while the stock rubber bonded engine mount attaches to the hole in the tubing.

Here's how the square tubing mount appears when used to mount a small block Chevy in a Toyota Landcruiser.

the mount situation involving installing the Belchfire Eight into the 1955 Zot. At this point the engine should be lowered into place and securely located with jacks, chain hoist, blocks of two-byfour and bailing wire (don't laugh—that's the way professional engine swappers do it). Regardless of welding experience or equipment you can now start to fabricate engine mounts! Sure! Get some light cardboard, a pencil, short ruler, scissors and tape and slide under the Zot and fabricate some mock-up mounts out of cardboard.

Here is a sound, and artistic touch given to a mount welded in an early Ford frame. A bolt will run through the stock mount on the block and into the tubing on the frame mount.

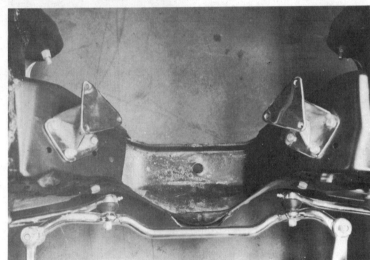

This is a competition setup which eliminates any rubber between engine and frame. The triangular pad bolts directly to the block.

Start by bolting a new set of stock engine mounts to the block. If it is at all possible, use the stock mounts for the reasons already outlined. With the new stock mounts in place start measuring and cutting cardboard to serve as a template for the mount you'll use to join the stock mounts to the frame. Do some thinking before wildly attacking the cardboard with the scissors. What is the simple, sanitary way to fashion the mounts? Can you use a piece of heavy wall square tubing with one hole drilled in it? Wouldn't this be a lot easier and faster than coming up with a design requiring flame-cut pieces and then welding them together? If welding cannot be done on the car at

this time, mounts will have to be fashioned so they can be bolted to the frame and the vehicle then driven to a welding shop.

When fabricating the templates of cardboard or stiff paper, keep in mind you should use mild steel with a thickness of not less than 3/16-inch when dealing with a full size engine. Once the mount templates are accurately done, they can be taken to a welding or machine shop to be made. If you make a detailed accurate drawing of the mounts with all dimensions clearly spelled out, the mounts will fit.

If stock type mounts cannot be used, then some sort of yoke cut from flat plate must be fashioned

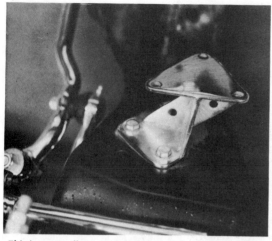

This is an excellent example of bracing a frame mount to eliminate any flexing although light metal is used for the construction.

This is the underside of a well constructed frame mount which bolts to a stock engine mount. Check that neat arc welding.

This is a three piece homemade mount used to locate a Buick in a '56 Ford pickup. Although the mount may appear to be elaborate, note that only flat strap was used.

Body shop vise grips are practically essential when mounts must be fabricated. Once you have a couple of sets around the garage, you'll find a zillion uses for them.

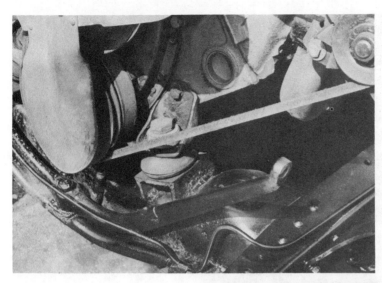

This is a crudely executed but effective method of mounting a small block Chevy in an early Ford truck using the early Ford rubber biscuit and the '55-'56 Chevy block mount.

This is a classic example of what not to do. It is difficult to say which is worse — the design or the execution. The result was a mount that failed.

Vehicles with unitized bodies offer the greatest challenge in fabricating mounts or crossmembers. This is a well done crossmember in a Mustang.

and bolted to the block. At the outer end of the yoke, there must be a small pad. Under the pad will go a "rubber biscuit" which in turn gets sandwiched on top of the frame mount. The rubber biscuit or insulator is readily available at auto parts stores because they were used to mount all flat head Ford V8 engines in cars and trucks from 1921 through 1953. There is no magic to building a good set of mounts. There is no secret formula and you don't have to be a master craftsman to get the job done. All of the mystery about making mounts will vanish if you will understand our section on phasing the engine and work with light cardboard to make templates of the mounting hardware. We've included a lot of photos in this section to show you a lot of good ideas concerning mounts and crossmembers.

This shot of the Mustang mount shows the ease of removing either the crossmember or the stock rubber mount. Simple construction makes this a simple mount to make.

When crossmembers must be dependant on sheet metal for support, make them as short and simple as possible and back up the bolts on the interior with plates or very large washers.

As more and more cars and trucks are constructed of unitized sheet metal, you'll be seeing more of this type of crossmember.

The exact method of execution can vary greatly but the best rule of thumb is to make it simple. This crossmember demonstrates that.

Pre-bent universal crossmembers are available for the engine swapper, or you can have a muffler shop bend something like this for you. First make a template of very heavy wire.

This is the stock transmission mount used on most of the GM transmissions. It's very effective and simple and that makes it easy to make a crossmember to accept it.

The stock crossmember works out OK in this swap—after the holes were slotted, but look how part of the subframe bracing had to be cut out to clear the shift rods.

These are three completely different examples of crossmembers used when putting late engines in early frames. Notice how one builder uses the crossmember to hold the transmission, locate the rear radius rods and serve as a bracket for the master cylinder—yet the member unbolts for easy servicing of any component. Now check the mount completely welded to the frame which means the engine will have to be pulled in order to remove the transmission.

The Exhaust System

Problems with the exhaust system need to be appraised with the same cold logic you use for sizing up all the other problems associated with an engine swap. What is practical for you? Your preliminary measurements should uncover obvious problems such as the outlet portion of the left exhaust manifold interfering with the steering box. Let's say the manifold will hit the steering box. What are your options in solving this problem? You can get another, different, exhaust manifold; the one you have can be modified; or special exhaust headers can be purchased or fabricated to clear the steering box.

Let's explore these options—and along the way you can make up your mind about the practicality of each choice for you. Through the production life of an engine perhaps a dozen different cast iron exhaust manifolds will be built. In the case of the small block Chevy, you can find a manifold for the left side that has the exhaust outlet at the very rear or near the center. By using a right side exhaust on the left side, you can have a manifold that will place the exhaust outlet at the front of the engine. The same holds true for many other engines. The parts man at a dealership can help out here, and so can a sharp guy at a wrecking yard. Solving the exhaust clearance problem with a stock part obviously has the advantage of being low in cost and quick. If you are primarily concerned with vehicle performance in your proposed swap, you probably won't want a cast iron manifold, though.

Some exhaust clearance problems can be solved by modifying a stock cast iron manifold. A cast iron manifold can be cut with a milling machine, a band saw or hacksaw. It can be welded in most welding shops. The outlet of the manifold can be moved from front to rear, or the side of the manifold moved inward just enough to provide the needed clearance. Unless you do your own cast iron welding, I would suggest that you talk the problem over with a welder before starting to hack up a manifold. He may want to do the cutting of the manifold so he will have better control of how the pieces fit when it all goes back together. He may want you to supply him with two manifolds—so a section of one can be grafted onto the other. A qualified welder can answer your specific questions about what can and cannot be done with a cast iron manifold to provide the clearance you need.

The third option in solving exhaust clearance

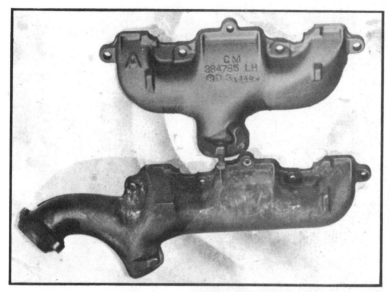

For many domestic engines there is more than one exhaust manifold for the same block. Both of these manifolds fit the small block Olds and are available from the parts counter of an Olds dealer.

If you plan to eliminate a cast iron manifold, check to see how many accessories hang from it. Overlooking this can make big problems out of little ones.

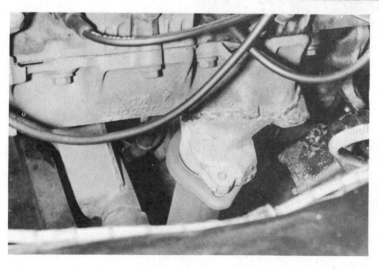

Here is a good example of a modified cast iron manifold. Note that the outlet did dump directly onto the steering box.

Regardless of type of exhaust system, maintain a minimum of 3/8-inch clearance between exhaust and frame or support structure to eliminate noise.

This is a neat approach to a dual exhaust system where space is limited. A very sanitary installation.

problems involves the use of headers. Headers are exhaust manifolds made of steel tubing instead of cast iron. Compared to the stock manifold, headers are light, lend themselves to sizeable gains in horsepower and are fashionable. Compared to cast iron manifolds, they are expensive. There are a dozen or so companies making headers for domestic and foreign cars and trucks. Many of these companies also manufacture header kits allowing the home builder to fabricate headers for a particular application.

First, let's take a look at the header you can buy in a speed shop or by mail order. In the first place a header is built for a particular engine installed by the factory in a particular car or truck. If you buy a header system you will be asked the year, make and model of car, size of engine, whether the vehicle is equipped with power steering and automatic transmission. In other words, the headers are built to fit a specifically named vehicle. This makes it rough—if not down right impossible for the engine swapper wanting a set of "out of the box" headers. You can't very well start buying set after set of headers and hauling them home to see if they will fit in your particular swap—and then taking them back (greasy and scratched up) when they don't work out. This leaves you with headers made just for a limited number of swaps. Some

manufacturers of engine swap hardware make headers for some swaps. This works out fine, but a word of caution is in order. Just because firm A offers headers for a small block Ford in a Pinto swap, do not assume you can build your own engine mounts, set the engine where you want it and then buy the headers and have them fit. No way. The headers that are built and sold to be used in engine swaps are built to be used with a particular set of engine mounts. Get the headers and mounts from the same firm.

"Do it yourself" header kits consist of gaskets, flanges, a quantity of straight and bent tubing, collectors and reducers. The tubing can be cut with tin snips or a hacksaw and obviously the tubing can be routed to clear most any obstruction. Obviously the tubing must be welded to the flange and then all of the little pieces of tubing on down the line must be welded together. This is a lot more time consuming and demanding of skill and patience than you might think if you've never built a set of headers before. Don't attempt the job unless you are a fair-to-middlin' gas welder.

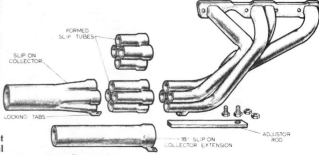

At least ½-inch clearance should be left between exhaust and steering box. Heat can cause steering box lube to boil and steering box to fail.

(Above) An adjustable header kit by Hooker. Below, Hooker's hot air package allows you to replace stock heat stove tube from header to air cleaner.

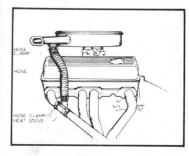

(Left) Putting a full size engine in a compact car almost always creates exhaust clearance problems such as this one with the Vega steering shaft.

Never attempt to build a set of headers for a vehicle until all engine mounting hardware is complete and the engine is firmly bolted down to where it will "live" in the car. Before getting carried away with cutting and welding tubing, I suggest you make a sketch of where you plan to rout the tubing. In the sketch, number the tubes up near where they mate with the head, and then number them again at the point they go into the collector. If you have never built a set of headers before, you won't understand the reason for this until you get under the vehicle for the 23rd time with a little piece of tubing in one hand and a hot torch in the other. I would also suggest you tack weld the entire header together before completing any welds. As you design your headers—either on paper, or on the car as you go—keep several things in mind: 1) Sooner or later you will want to change spark plugs. Don't lose sight of that in building the headers. 2) You must also provide access for a wrench on the flange bolts. 3) If at all possible, build the headers so they may be removed from the car without removing the engine or disassembling half of the suspension. On difficult swaps this is no easy task.

If you know that stock exhaust manifolds will not work—even if modified—and there are no headers readily available for your swap, and you can't weld, what do you do? At this point you simply fall back and do what is practical for you. Visit muffler shops in the area. State flatly what you have in mind. Can they, and will they, custom-build a set of headers for you? When you find a place willing to tackle the job, ask them if they want you to provide the complete header kit, or

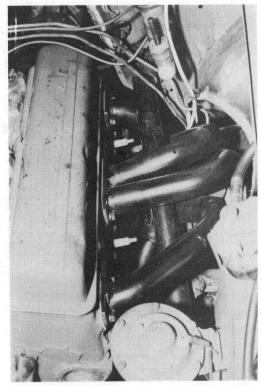

Fender well headers can often solve some exhaust problems. The drawback is that they don't look so hot and that they are often very difficult to install and remove.

only a flange kit—or nothing but the vehicle and the cash to pay the bill. I mention this because in addition to complete header kits, some companies offer flange kits for some of the more popular engines. These kits normally consist of a gasket, flange, flange bolts and swedged tubing to

This is a nice set of amateur built headers for a Chevy installed in an early Ford. Note how the flange has been cut between the last two cylinders so the header may easily be removed.

This set of headers was built by using a kit of bent tubing and other header components. The application is Ford into Jaguar.

This is an attempt to get a set of store-bought headers to fit an other than stock location. The rear tube has almost been hammered closed and still comes very close to the steering box. Muffler shop surgery could cure this problem.

When constructing your own header system, it may facilitate things to remove the starter. Just don't forget to leave room for the starter—and it would be nice to be able to remove and replace the unit without having to remove the exhaust system.

A muffler shop can fix you up with several sizes of flanges which can be used to make certain sections of the exhaust system readily removable in order to service other components.

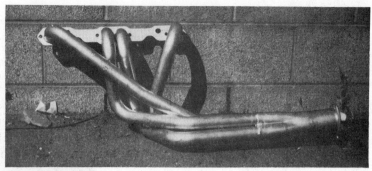

This is a prime example of why store bought headers cannot be counted on to solve exhaust clearance problems in an engine swap. Both of these headers fit the same engine, but different cars.

mate with the flange. The tubing provided in a kit like this is normally only one to three inches long, which means you or the muffler shop has to come up with the rest of the tubing, collector pipe, reducer and the rest of the exhaust system. Some muffler shops can handle this, some can't.

Normally, there are two or more shops in every metropolitan area that actually specialize in custom exhaust systems.

BEYOND THE MANIFOLD OR HEADER

Many shops which specialize in doing engine swaps on a custom basis do not fabricate the exhaust system in back of the header or exhaust manifold. The reasoning behind this is quite simple—a good man in a muffler shop with all the hardware and tools at hand can do everything on an exhaust system so much better and quicker than the average individual that it simply doesn't make sense to attempt to hang mufflers and tailpipe yourself, unless it is aboslutely necessary.

FROM HOME TO MUFFLER SHOP— HOW DO YOU GET THERE?

If you promise not to sue me or haul me into court as the culprit who influenced your life

against the law, I'll level with you. In very few of the engine swaps I've done or helped with, has the exhaust system been complete at the time the car was otherwise ready to drive. As noted elsewhere in this volume, I'm a firm believer in letting radiator shops do radiator work and muffler shops do muffler work. Therefore, I have transported a number of vehicles with an "open" exhaust (no mufflers) to various muffler shops in order to get the job completed. At this point, I will not make suggestions—only the following observations:

— Most states require that a towed vehicle be towed behind a vehicle so equipped for towing (like a wrecker) or a vehicle legally equipped for towing (like another car with a trick hitch and all the legal wiring) and sometimes a towing permit.

— As far as I know, all states require a muffler on all vehicles driven on public roads.

— I've never been cited for driving a vehicle with open exhaust to a muffler shop.

A number of header manufacturers sell mandrel built U-bends of various sizes and radii to help the home builder construct a set of headers.

— When driving a vehicle with open exhaust to a muffler shop, I've always had a passenger. The passenger looked out the back window while I looked out the front.

— On the one occassion when I encountered a law enforcement officer while driving a vehicle with open exhausts, I turned the ignition switch to the "off" position. When the officer approached, my only explanation for stalling in the intersection was that I had run out of gas.

Collectors can also be purchased from header companies. They are available in various sizes and lengths.

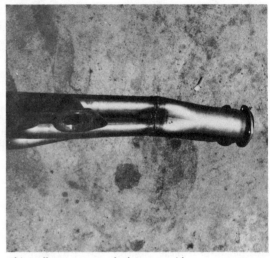

This collector was cocked to one side on purpose — to clear a chassis component. This is easy to do before the header system is completely welded together. Tack first — then fit.

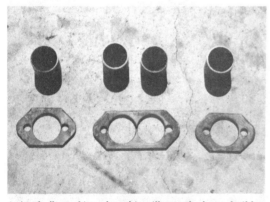

A simple flange kit such as this will save the home builder a lot of hours in building headers. These kits are readily available.

Rear Axle Swapping

Generally speaking, a full size rear axle should be used with a "full size engine". By that, I mean if you are installing a small block Chevy in a Toyota, then an axle originally meant to handle the horsepower of a small block Chevy should be installed in the car. The axle need not be from a Chevy but it should be of sufficient size to handle the horsepower of the Chevy—which means you could choose an axle from any full size sedan. There are always exceptions to rules in the world of engine swapping and you just might be able to do an engine swap without changing axles. If the car is to be driven carefully and equipped with an automatic transmission, then the stock axle can often be retained. This is especially true if a larger engine is installed in an intermediate size car. Normally the stock rear axle can be retained in a pickup truck if a larger than stock engine is installed.

Larger brakes and increased reliability are two benefits of swapping axles. Expense and labor are a couple of drawbacks. Swapping axles can get just as involved as swapping engines unless you think things through and—once again—determine what is practical for you. Installing a large axle in a small car often means the axle has to be narrowed. This is a job for a large machine shop and it goes something like this. It must first be determined how wide the axle must be in order to fit under the fenders of the car. The axle assembly is then taken apart and the axle housing is cut into on both sides of the differential, shortened and

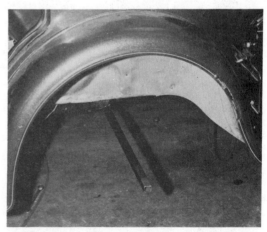

Before getting carried away with a lot of fabricating involving rear axle replacement, it's a good idea to C-clamp a piece of steel in place to serve as a reference point for any measurements that might be needed.

If you'll look at the third member housing carefully, you'll see these two rear axles are essentially the same. Different hardware has been attached in order to mount leaf springs on one and coil springs on the other. Width and wheel bolt patterns may also be different.

the pinion when the rear axle is hung from dual leaf springs by using an axle wedge between the axle mounting pad and the spring. Wedges come in various sizes and angles and can be bought from frame alignment shops. If coil springs are used, then the pinion angle can be changed by altering the length of the control arms or by relocating the control arm bracket on the axle housing. This latter step is best left to a competent frame alignment shop.

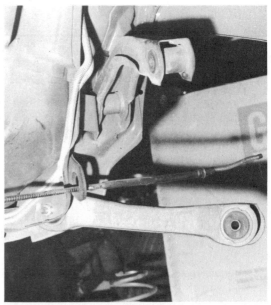

On late model cars using links to locate the axle in a fore and aft position, it's a good idea to leave them in place and . . .

welded back together. The axle shafts are then shortened and re-splined and the assembly is bolted back together. Not every machine shop is capable of this, so you may need to do some shopping around before locating a capable shop.

If the axle doesn't need to be narrowed, chances are good it still might need to be modified in some way before it can be placed under the car. If the larger axle was originally used with coil springs and the car it is going into has leaf springs, then it is pretty obvious something will have to be changed. Generally it is easier to change the spring and shock brackets on the axle than it is to completely change the spring set-up in the rear of the car. Predicate your choice on what is practical for you.

If you do not have the capability of cutting and welding, then you should think through the process of having a machine shop shorten the axle (if it is needed) and then changing the mounting hardware on the axle housing to be compatable with the rear suspension system of the car. In some cases you may have to leave all brackets off the axle housing until the engine is phased and the correct angle of the pinion can be determined. Some minor changes can be made in the angle of

. . . fabricate new brackets on the new axle which align with the stock links.

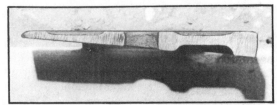

Frame alignment shops have alignment wedges like this one which can be placed between spring pack and spring pad to alter pinion angle slightly.

BUYING AN AXLE

Buying a rear axle for swapping purposes should be carried out somewhat like buying an engine — take your time and do a lot of shopping. There are more axles around than there are guys wanting to buy them. If possible, find the axle that will suit your needs still installed in a car. Check the odometer for miles and check the general condition of the car to see if it appeared to have been cared for before being centerpunched and hauled off to the wrecking yard. On many late model cars a complete list of options and accessories is stuck on an inner fender panel under the hood. If the car was equipped with a limited slip differential, this will be noted on the option list. The same goes for an optional ratio. Although this is not a sure fire way of finding out about the rear axle, it works 99% of the time. On some rear axles a plastic or metal tag is attached to the lube fill plug which proclaims that only special limited slip lubricant be used. This method of identifying or locating a limited slip axle also works about 99% of the time. The only sure way of determining ratio and the existence of limited slip is to pull the inspection cover or remove the differential carrier from the axle housing so the number of teeth of the gears can be counted and the differential inspected for the limited slip hardware. Some wrecking yards will allow this; some won't. Some wrecking yards will guarantee a rear axle not to be noisy; some won't. Obviously, if you narrow the axle and torch all the brackets off the housing in order to fit a particular application, a wrecking yard could hardly be expected to take an axle back — noise or no noise.

Like buying an engine, buy an axle assembly complete and you'll save money in the long run. Get both drums and the driveshaft and don't let "Cutting Torch Charlie" nip off the emergency brake cables a couple of inches away from the backing plates. Get all of the shielded cable and as much of the open cable as you can.

This Jaguar rear axle has been cleaned off and stripped of all unneeded hardware — ready to be mounted in a roadster. This gets to be more involved than most amateurs can handle.

Electrical supply firms carry cable clamping devices which are ideal for clamping emergency brake cables together.

One final word is in order before leaving this section on rear axle swapping. Chances are better than even that as you change rear axles you'll be changing the wheel bolt pattern. In other words, the wheels on your old rear axle will not bolt to the new assembly due to a difference in the bolt

Axles are removed in wrecking yards by the fastest method possible — a cutting torch. Note how the leaf spring was sliced into, even with the spring pad on this Camaro axle.

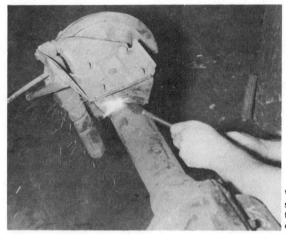

circle diameter or possibly the number of bolts needed to attach the wheel to the drum. Normally, the simple way to solve the problem is have the axle flanges and drums on the rear re-drilled to match the wheels. This eliminates having to carry two spare tires—one for the front and one for the rear. Most any machine shop is capable of altering the bolt pattern and pressing in new studs which are readily available from auto parts houses.

When removing any hardware from an axle housing, make sure you don't cut a hole in the housing. If this is done, the axles will have to be removed and the hole welded close.

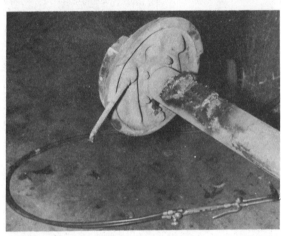

At this point it is far better to lay down the torch—rather than risk buring a hole in the axle housing in order to remove a little more of the bracket.

Larger sections of bracket that are electric welded to the housing can be removed with hammer and chisel.

The remainder of brackets and slag can be removed with a hand held grinder.

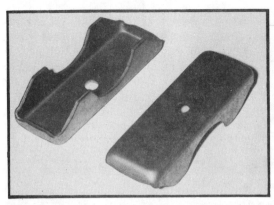

Speed shops normally carry spring pads such as this which can be welded to any live axle housing.

Universal spring pads are normally stamped for the smallest of axle housing diameters . . . and thus won't fit every housing without some work. Note how this pad doesn't fit the housing . . . .

. . . but does after grinder has been put to work on the pad mating surface.

Emergency brake cables from the new axle can easily be clamped to the cables already in the car with these industrial electric wiring clamps.

Don't make things more complicated than they need to be. Check that shock mounting bracket at top.

Approaching Oil System Problems

In some swaps, the oil system is a major problem area—in others there is not a hint of trouble. Before actually getting into a swap though, you should realize there can be a problem here and you should have a grasp on how to go about solving the problems. Then make a judgment as to what is practical for you in terms of solving the problems. Two problems commonly arise—the oil filter gets in the way of the frame or a crossmember or the pan become "an interference fit" with a crossmember or some steering gear component. There is no need for panic—both problems can be solved.

First, let's take a look at oil filters. Depending on the engine, they can be located at the front, or rear, on the side of the block. Those at the rear of the block seem to give less trouble in swapping than those in other locations, but rear mounted filters are not immune to problems with rerouted exhaust systems—necessary to clear steering appendages. Let's say the very end of the filter comes in contact with some part of the chassis. What do you do? The first move is to figure out if the side of the filter or the end of it is creating the problem. If the end of the filter is hitting the header, frame, crossmember, or whatever; trundle off to the parts counter at the dealership having parts for the engine. Present the problem to the parts man and find out if there is a shorter filter for the engine you have. For instance, there are four separate lengths of spin-on filters that I know of for small block Chevys. The longest is 9½-inches and the shortest is just over 4-inches. By going to a shorter filter, the filtering capacity is reduced—but that just means you change filters more often. Big deal, if it solves the interference problem for you in a swap!

If the side of the filter is coming into contact with some part of the chassis, the name of the game changes. You could eliminate part of the chassis so the filter will clear. Give it a lot of thought. As we have pointed out earlier, the factory doesn't put a crossmember or frame in for looks. Light a torch and remove a part of a frame and you'll destroy some of the structural integrity. If a small notch or a large dimple with a ball peen hammer will solve the problem, that's one thing—but cutting away a large piece of frame or crossmember is a sure-fire way of ruining a swap (and maybe a vehicle) for most swappers.

There are several varieties of remote oil filter holders. This one worked out well on the inner center panel when the stock filter interfered with the frame.

Chevrolet has two in-out adapters for the small block V8 which allow a cooler to be plumbed from the fitting. Regular filter spins on the end.

The other choice in eliminating filter interference problems is to move the filter. This is a simple, low cost way out of a difficult problem. Moving the filter location is done routinely by professional engine swappers and those who build race cars, but for some reason unknown to me, the amateur seems to shy away from this very obvious solution. Several companies manufacture oil filter block-off plates. These are machined cast aluminum plates that bolt on where the oil filter normally fits. Each plate has provision for two pipe fittings—one inlet and one exit for oil flowing to a remotely mounted filter. When a block-off plate is used, a second machined casting is used to hold the oil filter. Oil lines are merely routed from casting number one to casting number two—which holds the oil filter. All of this is a matter of simple plumbing and you can mount the filter on an inner fender panel or the firewall. If you like, a cooler can be mounted between filter mounting

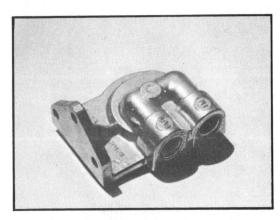

Here's an in-out adapter which allows a remote-mounted filter to be mounted in position.

and the line back to the block. Without a doubt, this is THE sanitary way out of a filter interference problem. Filter block-off plates and filter mounting bosses carry instructions as to what size, and what type of plumbing to use when remotely mounting the filter. READ THE INSTRUCTIONS! An old piece of fuel line and some twisted bailing wire for a clamp simply wasn't designed for 50 pounds of oil pressure.

Under no circumstances should you attach an oil filter block-off plate to an engine and then plug the inlet and outlet lines! Eliminating the filter from the oiling system of a modern day engine makes about as much sense as eating soup with a knife!

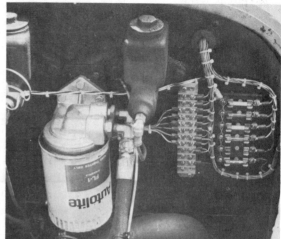

(Above) Here's an easy way to get to filter installation on the firewall of a Jeep. Man, check that super neat wiring!

(Top left) Here's a case where the stock filter clears, but may be more trouble than it's worth when changing time comes.

[Bottom left] An in-between length filter for a small block Ford which allows for plenty of room for servicing.

(Below) If the room is available for a larger than stock filter, you might ask the parts man what he has in the way of an extra capacity filter for your engine. Both these filters fit a small block Chevy. Small filter is stock size. AC unit is for a large truck, but will fit in many passenger car installations.

Oil filters are available in a variety of lengths for most domestic engines. This super short filter for a small block Ford just does clear the inside of an early Ford frame.

OIL PANS

Problems with oil pans don't come up any more often in swapping than problems with filters—they're just more difficult to solve, and the level of skill needed to solve the problem is far more critical. Crossmembers and tie rods interfere with oil pans—and in some badly planned swaps the axle will get in the way of the pan. On these pages there are numerous examples of how pans can be reshaped to provide the needed clearance. For the most of us, this is not as simple as it might appear.

The first step you should take in solving a clearance problem is to determine just how much of an interference there is. If the leading edge of the sump just barely touches a crossmember, then some judicious work on the pan with a hammer and a dolly might solve the problem. At the same time, if the trailing edge of the crossmember has a lip on it, perhaps this can be ground away with a

body grinder to offer the necessary clearance.

If the pan is clearly the wrong shape for the chassis, then you will be faced with finding a pan of a different shape or having one made. Several size and shape pans are often available for an engine. For instance, most small block Fords use a pan with a front sump. As you might imagine, this causes all sorts of grief in a lot of swaps. However, when the small block Ford is used in a Bronco, a rear sump pan is used—and knowing this can quickly solve a problem at a very low cost. This is the sort of information available from friendly parts men at dealerships and from wrecking yards. When using a pan other than the one coming on your engine, it is imperative that you use the oil pickup assembly and dipstick designed for the pan!

The last resort in solving a pan clearance problem is to severly reshape a stock item. There are more problems associated with this than you

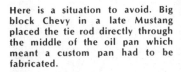

Here is a situation to avoid. Big block Chevy in a late Mustang placed the tie rod directly through the middle of the oil pan which meant a custom pan had to be fabricated.

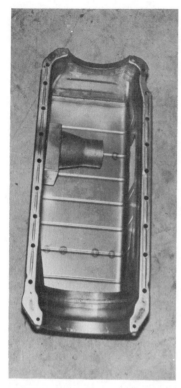

(Left and above) Custom oil pan to allow passage of the tie rod should be tried on the engine and in the car several times before welding is completed.

might think. In the first place, an oil pan is a relatively thin piece of metal. Normally a pan is reinforced only at the lip where it bolts to the block and in the drain plug area. When you start slicing away on a pan, it gets pretty flimsy. When you start to weld on it, the pan begins to warp. Then when you try to bolt it back on the block, it won't fit. Get the picture? To make matters even worse, a pan is difficult to weld on for the amateur welder since the metal is thin. This means the finished product is liable to leak. When oil gets hot and the pressure builds up in the crankcase, the lube will begin seeping through the weld. At this point you can get pretty unhappy—especially

if you have to pull the engine in order to remove the pan and start all over with the welding.

If it becomes necessary to severely reshape a pan, I suggest the following procedure. Make a cardboard or tin template of the existing pan profile. Lower the engine into the chassis and place it exactly where you want it. Now put the template in place against the bottom of the block and trim the template to the shape the pan should be. Remove the trimmed template and transfer the shape to the oil pan. Before cutting the pan—with a saber saw and tin snips—determine where you will locate the pickup assembly if any of the cutting is in this area and determine how you will gain back the original capacity of the pan if the surgery is to be severe. Never figure you'll just run the engine with less oil and never figure you'll just run the level of oil higher since this will most likely place the level of the oil into the crank throws. Do some thinking before you do any cutting. Once you have cut the pan, bolt it to the block and lower the engine back into the chassis, making sure it is in the correct location. If your cutting has provided you with the correct clearance, metal can now be shaped, trimmed, clamped in place and welded. For the inexperienced welder,

When an oil pan is altered, don't overlook possible modifications to oil pump pickup, dipstick and dipstick brace.

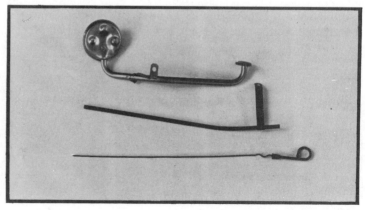

When an oil pan is notched to provide clearance for a
steering component, make sure there is plenty of clearance as the wheel is turned and the suspension is compressed and then released. In other words, is this tie rod going to hit the oil pan if the vehicle hits a large bump and then picks one front wheel off the ground?

This is an oil pan looking for a place to leak! Oil pan has less than ¼-inch clearance with the front axle. To remedy the situation, the engine was pulled and a new pan fabricated by an engine swap shop. Color the oil pan green for the amount of money it took to fix.

this is far more complicated than it sounds. Arc welding tends to burn through the thin metal, gas welding warps the metal. Those who modify oil pans for a living use heli-arc—which you are not likely to have. For the amateur, the best bet is to use gas and do the welding with the pan bolted in place on the block. If you are a pretty fair gas welder, the following procedure can be used when welding an oil pan. Assuming the engine is assembled, wrap the exposed crank and rod assembly in dry or oily shop rags. Then place a layer of wet shop rags in the pan and bolt the pan to the block with the block laying on its side or standing upright on the bellhousing. With the pan securely bolted to the block to reduce warpage, the pan can now be welded. The oily or dry rags keep slag, flux, and so on, from falling down into the engine, and the wet rags make sure the oily or dry rags don't catch on fire.

Here is a case of a stock pan needing to be altered just slightly to provide plenty of clearance for a front crossmember. Note unfinished header still to be completed once engine is mounted in place.

After completing the welding, remove the pan from the engine and clean the inside of it thoroughly. Then test it for leaks by pouring in several quarts of warm automatic transmission fluid. Make sure the fluid thoroughly covers the welded area. Let the pan hold the oil for several hours before making a judgment it doesn't leak. A leak in an oil pan doesn't go away . . . it just continues to leak. And usually, vibration from the engine will make a small leak grow.

Any modification to any oil pan should be made with consideration for the oil pump pickup. Never lose sight of the simple fact that the pickup assembly must be covered with more than an inch of oil at all times or it runs the danger of sucking a vortex in the lube and ingesting a quantity of air. When this happens, rod and main bearings fail. Pickup tubes can be shortened, lengthened and reshaped. Just make sure the tube doesn't leak, and that there are no leaks at the junction with the pump or at the pickup. Although the pickup should always be covered with oil, don't shove it completely down against the bottom of the pan. There should be 3/8-inch between the bottom of the pan and the bottom of the pickup.

There are some swaps requiring reworked pans that are so common, modified pans are already available from firms who handle engine swapping hardware. Though the cost of the modified pan may seem high, it is really very low when compared to the amount of work and frustration involved in doing it yourself.

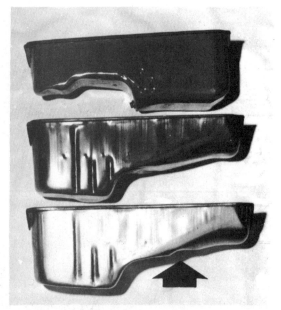

Several pans are made for most engines. Here are three available for the small block Chevy. Note the subtle differences in the bottom two. Knowing about the availability of the bottom pan could solve a clearance problem in a hurry. The front sump pan at the top [early Nova] could mean the difference between doing the swap and not doing it.

(Above) Small tabs tack welded inside altered pan help to keep oil from running forward during braking so pickup tube remains covered with lube.

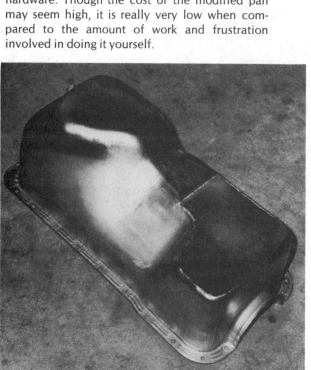

(Left) A slight modification such as this alters pan capacity an insignificant amount.

Cooling System

THE MORE RADICAL THE SWAP,
THE MORE DIFFICULT THE PROBLEM

Solving cooling problems should start while planning the swap—not while tapping the temperature guage the first time you take your pride and joy around the block. Keeping the operating temperature of an engine down to an acceptable level during all phases of operation can become unbelievably complicated—not just for the engine swapper, but for the automotive engineer. We have personal knowledge of a large firm that went broke simply because their fleet of trucks constantly overheated. Not even the factory that built the trucks could solve the problem until it was too late. The engines boiled over, pistons seized, heads cracked and cargo shipments were delayed —all because of chronic overheating. An overheating problem is not necessarily solved simply by increasing the size of the radiator. Overheating is far more complicated.

When doing an engine swap—or planning one— keep in mind the capacity and the area of the radiator used should be close to what the engine was mated with in it's original application. For instance, the specification chart on a small block

Chevy V8 used in a Chevelle might spell out that the cooling system had a capacity of 12 quarts. The radiator might have 300 square inches of area (length times width). Obviously, you are looking

In any swap remove the radiator before pulling out the old engine. This prevents a water pump shaft from punching an expensive hole in the middle of the core. If the stock radiator will not be used in the swap, it can probably be sold to lower the overall cost of the project.

One of the most popular radiators being used in swaps today is the crossflow Corvette unit which is small, easy to mount and provides excellent cooling for the largest of engines.

Most modern radiators rest on some sort of support rather than being held in place with bolts along a side flange. A support like this can easily be made from a piece of channel.

Here is a case where a simple support bar was made from a piece of square tubing. Each end bolts to an inner fender panel to keep sheet metal in alignment as well as provide a place to mount an upper support clamp.

for problems if you install the Chevy in an MG and cut the coolant capacity to 6 quarts and the radiator area to 100 square inches. You might get away with this in Anchorage, Alaska but problems are sure to develop in August in Gila Bend, Arizona.

Thus the first rule of thumb in heading off cooling problems is to come close in capacity and radiator area to what the engine originally lived with. This may mean some major surgery on the front interior sheetmetal in order to fit a radiator of the proper size—and this may not be practical for you. Never lose sight of that—what's practical for you?

A competent radiator shop can build most any size or shape radiator you need and it is wise to locate such a shop before hacking away at the

To prevent chafing, rubber should be used between the bottom of the radiator and the supporting structure. Simple clamping bracket at the top keeps radiator from moving.

An upper support clamp holding a Chevrolet radiator being used in a 1951 Ford truck.

swap without giving any thought to cooling. For instance, in the case just mentioned, a good radiator shop might recommend that you double the thickness of the core used in the MG instead of making the radiator taller or wider.

Don't lose sight of how a modern cooling system works. The engine water pump pumps hot water out of the engine and into the radiator, air flowing through the radiator removes heat from the water, and the cooled water flows back into the engine. The key to the effectiveness of this system is the flow of air. A radiator 9 feet tall and 6 feet wide wouldn't cool a small block Chevy unless there was a flow of air through the radiator. Due to the increased capacity of the system, it might take a while before all of the water got hot, but when it did you would be faced with 50 gallons of water at 250 degrees instead of 3 gallons at the same temperature. The water may be pulling the heat from the engine, but the heat must be transferred from the water to the air if cooling is to be effective. This means the flow of air into the radiator and out of the radiator must be efficient—and this is where things can get complicated in a hurry if an overheating problem

does come up. We say "if" because in the vast majority of engine swaps matching coolant capacity and radiator area to the engine solves the problem. You need not be frightened out of doing a swap because there is a very remote chance you'll have cooling problems.

As you are planning the swap consider the following steps of the cooling process. A very small grille opening can restrict the amount of air going into the radiator. If the grille opening is a foot or more from the radiator, air trapped just behind the grille can build up turbulence and keep more air from entering. Sometimes this can be solved by reducing the cavity area between the grille and radiator and forming a front shroud which moves air immediately from grille to radiator. In other cases, the grille opening might simply be too small and will have to be enlarged or air will have to be ducted to the radiator from shrouding under the bumper. At low vehicle speed or while idling in traffic, air flow through the radiator can be increased by using a fan of increased pitch, by using a fan with more blades, or by installing a shroud around the fan at the back of the radiator. Air flowing out the back of the radiator still has to have a place to go. On your proposed swap, how will the hot air exit the engine compartment? This matters a great deal. If the air cannot get out of the engine compartment, pressure begins to build up—even to the point it

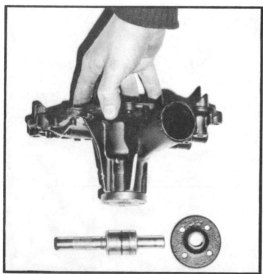

(Above and below) Most water pumps can be shortened by a machinist. The nose of the pump housing will be cut down and a shortened shaft installed. Sometimes even the mounting flange for the fan can be narrowed to provide the needed amount of clearance.

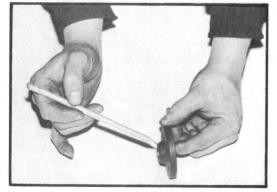

may try to get back out of the engine compartment via the radiator! It is simple to assume the air wants to flow back alongside the engine and down the firewall to the leading edge of the floorboard where it will be swept from beneath the car by all of the air flowing beneath the car at road speed. Don't count on this if you've packed the engine compartment full. How much clearance is there between the back of the engine and the firewall? How much clearance is there between the bellhousing/transmission assembly and the floor? How much clearance is there between the exhaust system and the steering box or the inner fender panels? Lack of exits for the heated air can create some very real heating problems. Normally the problem is quickly solved by punching louvers in the hood or cutting openings in the inner fender panels. Solving a serious overheating problem can be a very frustrating and time consuming project. I was once hired to help solve the overheating problems on a prototype sports car. Cockpit temperature quickly got out of hand due to the proximity of the engine to the driver. The engine coolant temperature was barely acceptable at road speed and reached the boil-over point in about two minutes of idling. The vehicle was heavily instrumented and more than two dozen thermocouples were placed under the hood and in the cockpit area. After two weeks of recording data and making changes, two modifications showed more promise than any others. The rear of the engine was lowered to provide more room between the transmission/bellhousing assembly and the body of the car. This provided more exit area for the air leaving the radiator. This lowered

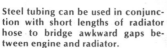

Steel tubing can be used in conjunction with short lengths of radiator hose to bridge awkward gaps between engine and radiator.

Here is a case of too much room being between fan and radiator. The radiator can be moved back, a shroud built from radiator to fan or the fan spaced forward.

Auto parts stores have fan spacers in a great variety of dimensions.

underhood air temperatures, coolant temperature and cockpit temperature. Unfortunately this made little change in how long it took for the engine to boil over at idle. A very low dam, or spoiler, was placed beneath the radiator to prevent air leaving

the engine compartment from flowing back through the radiator while the car was stopped! Two weeks of running tests and making changes was distilled into making two simple modifications—neither of which was even thought of when the job began!

Don't overlook the obvious when chasing an overheating problem. Is the radiator and water passages in the engine "clean" and unobstructed? Is the thermostat working? Take it out, throw it in a pan of boiling water and see if it opens. Is the fan within one inch of the back of the radiator? Does the air have a hard time getting from the grille opening to the radiator? Does the air have a hard time leaving the engine compartment? If you suspect it does, remove the hood and take note of

Regardless of mounting structure, a radiator should not be allowed to move. Often, simple bracing can be used to solve problems.

temperatures while running at road speed and while idling.

In recent years small radiators called "transmission coolers" have become popular. These transmission coolers are normally mounted just in front of the radiator and lines are then routed to carry transmission fluid back and forth from cooler to transmission. This effectively lowers the operating temperature of the automatic transmission. This is good because the lower operating temperature means longer life for the clutch material in the transmission. Where is the heat going? The flow of

(Left) Here is a good example of what can be done to make sure all air entering the grille passes through the radiator. Note the remote mounted Corvette fill tank.

(Below) This is race car stuff that would be right at home on the street. Duct work has been fabricated around an engine oil cooler to insure a forced flow of air through the cooler.

air through the cooler picks up the heat. This is the same air that then must flow through the radiator. When possible, mount a transmission cooler to one side or beneath a radiator and fabricate simple aluminum duct work to keep the flow of air through the trans cooler from going through the engine radiator. This simple move might not solve an overheating problem, but it might help. Three or four small moves such as this might completely solve the problem.

At one time 5 to 7 pound pressure caps on radiators were common; now 12 to 15 pound pressure caps are common. The boiling point of water is raised approximately 2.5 degrees Fahrenheit per pound of pressure. In other words, if you are chugging along in a Model A with no radiator cap at sea level the boiling point of the water is 212 degrees. If you clamped a 15 pound pressure cap on, the temperature of the water would have to rise to 257 degrees before it would boil. This is good to know because increasing the pressure of

This is not the best mounting location for a remotely mounted transmission oil cooler – but it works.

Many an air conditioning condenser has been turned into a transmission oil cooler. This one is angled slightly and mounted under the floor of a car sporting a recently swapped engine.

Most vehicle manufacturers offer several fans for each engine. Often a slight cooling problem can be solved by using a fan with more blades for increased air flow through the radiator at low speed.

Some foreign cars use electric fans to pull air through the radiator. This is one adapted to hot rod application. This worked fine for an already cool running Chevy.

Electric fans can be used to push the air through a radiator instead of pull it—which was the only solution in this crowded engine compartment.

Remote mounted filler and coolant recovery bottle is used on this Kelmark installation of a V8 in the backseat area of a Corvair.

Fill tank can be used to solve clearance problems. Corvette tanks are often used and are readily available from the Chevy parts counter. Note electric fan used here.

the cooling system can help solve an overheating problem, but don't clamp on a 15 pound pressure cap without taking the radiator (and preferably the vehicle) to a competent radiator shop to have the system pressure checked. Some radiators were simply not designed to take 15 pounds of pressure and will rupture and leak as the pressure goes up. Then you've really got an overheating problem!

Never attempt to solve an overheating problem by removing the thermostat. The function of the thermostat is to restrict the flow of water from the engine to the radiator while the engine is cold. This helps the engine to warm up faster which in turn cuts down on sludge and acid formation in the crankcase. By removing the thermostat, it is possible to create a situation where an engine always runs too cold. This in turn leads to a very high rate of wear on internal parts and decreased gas mileage. Make sure the thermostat is in good working order, then put it back where it belongs.

Probably the most important fact to leave with you in closing out this section is that overheating problems can be solved; but never assume it can be done simply by installing a larger radiator.

Curved, straight and flex hose comes in a jillion sizes and lengths and some careful picking can go a long way towards making a swapped engine look like it grew there.

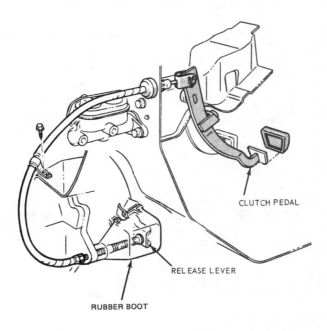

CLUTCH PEDAL

RELEASE LEVER

RUBBER BOOT

Clutch Linkage

Being upside down on a cold garage floor with a drop light searing the skin on one forearm trying to figure out how to build clutch linkage is the best reason I know for using nothing but an automatic transmission in all swaps. Professional engine swapper Andy Herbert says most guys simply do not possess the knowledge or skills to construct clutch linkage from scratch without having it bind some—or all of the time. If binding is not a problem, it might take a full grown gorilla to depress the pedal without straining. This last point can also put a considerable strain on marriage if the wife is also expected to drive the vehicle. Seriously consider an automatic transmission to completely eliminate the clutch linkage hassle.

Attempting to hook up clutch linkage can really turn into a head-scratching situation unless the swapper is aware of linkage rato and what it does to pedal effort and the total travel of the throwout arm. Try this one on for size. Current swing pedals usually reach the throwout arm only after transferring motion against a pedal return spring and through a pedal push rod (running through the firewall) to the ball-mounted cross shaft, then to the fork push rod, then to the clutch fork and

throwout bearing. Got that? This not only sounds complicated—but is when you start trying to modify some of it in order to actuate the clutch behind your new engine.

When building or modifying clutch linkage which hinges from engine and frame, the first step is to establish the pivot ball on the engine side to prevent binding when under load. With steering, exhaust and clutch work, this swap still has a long way to go.

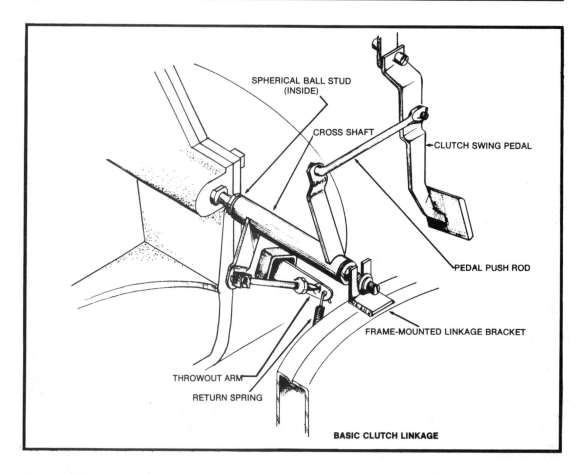

SPHERICAL BALL STUD
(INSIDE)

CROSS SHAFT

CLUTCH SWING PEDAL

PEDAL PUSH ROD

FRAME-MOUNTED LINKAGE BRACKET

THROWOUT ARM

RETURN SPRING

BASIC CLUTCH LINKAGE

We suggest you study the stock clutch linkage long and hard before removing any of it from the car to start the engine swap. Don't get red faced when I suggest you make a drawing of what goes where. Never, ever, throw one piece of linkage away until you have the car running for a week or so. Don't try to clean up the engine compartment, frame rails, etc. by torching off brackets having anything to do with clutch linkage.

The plan is to maintain just as much of the stock linkage as possible. After the engine and transmission are in place and mounted where they are supposed to be in the chassis, go to work on the clutch linkage. Do this before getting into the exhaust system. Give yourself all of the room possible under there. Crawl under and attack the problem from the standpoint of finding the simplest, most direct method of actuating the clutch with stock—or nearly stock—components. Andy Herbert summed it up quite well by saying in 999 cases out of 1,000, the further from stock a guy goes with clutch linkage, the worse it will be.

Never lose sight of the fact the engine is free to move slightly from side to side in the chassis—and

the clutch linkage is partially anchored to the engine and partially anchored to the chassis. For this reason, the side of the block is fitted with a ball stud from which the cross shaft may rotate— even when the engine is torqued over in the

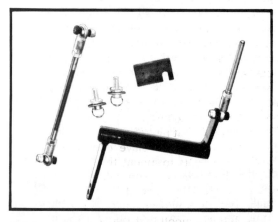

This is a universal clutch linkage kit made by Speedway Engineering, 2471 Fletcher Dr., Los Angeles, Calif. It fits a wide variety of applications. Check with them for details.

This is a straightforward use of a hydraulic slave unit to actuate the clutch. The very sturdy, direct line mounting is most important.

chassis. The ball stud and socket fitment into the cross shaft must be maintained. The shaft itself may be modified—shortened, off-set or whatever —but this vital, flexible link between chassis and drivetrain must be maintained. If it is not, the clutch will not release part of the time, or may partially release itself part of the time, or may partially release all of the time, or any of the above plus some other weird happenings.

An increasing number of vehicles are now equipped with hydraulic clutch linkage—thus it might seem this is the way out of having to put up with mechanical, problem-ridden hardware. For the amateur, a hydraulic clutch carries it's own set of nightmares. All of the clutch master cylinders currently available mount to the firewall and are operated by a swing pedal hanging from some pretty substantial brackets attached to the firewall and dash. When the amateur tries to transfer all of this to an older vehicle—originally equipped with the clutch and brake pedal running through the floor—all or part of the firewall bracing is eliminated and the master cylinder mounts directly to the firewall. This arrangement normally leads to a flexing firewall. As time goes on the amount of flex will increase to the point that pedal effort will flex the firewall but not release the clutch. Similar problems arise at the slave cylinder when the amateur attempts to mount the cylinder to the block or bell housing with a hastily conceived, poorly executed bracket. If a vehicle is already equipped with a hydraulic clutch, the installation will go rather smoothly if the master cylinder is left intact and the matching slave cylinder is used.

If you are very familiar with the principles of

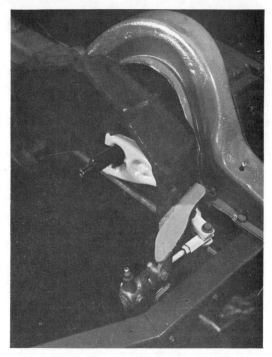

The Kelmark kit for mounting a V8 in a Corvair also uses a juice clutch effectively. Note the straight push and very sturdy mount to eliminate any flex.

The bent link between throwout arm and clutch rod may seem simple here, but when the piece is missing and the problem is all yours, an automatic transmission would be a real blessing.

mechanical engineering and can fabricate or tell someone else what to fabricate—clutch linkage is no problem. If this is not the case, I strongly suggest using an automatic transmission. Study the drawings, study the photos and decide before you get half way into the swap—that's the practical way of doing it.

This is a "universal" hydraulic clutch pedal assembly marketed by Advance Adapters.

Throttle Linkage

Throttle linkage is one of those small areas of a swap that never gets any thought until the last minute. Then, with the engine bolted in place and the exhaust system completed, the amateur is forced to solve the throttle linkage problem in a compromised manner. If this leads to binding in the linkage, or a throttle that won't open all the way, or a pedal requiring a lot of effort—then you are going to be unhappy. An otherwise successful swap can turn into an unhappy experience if the throttle linkage "just never quite works out."

Prior to 1949, most cars used a firewall mounted bell-crank to transfer pedal motion to the carb. This worked reasonably well in those older cars but this bell crank and rod linkage is the most difficult to modify in a swap. Most all cars and trucks built after about 1960 use a sheathed cable between pedal and carb. This is the most versatile and easiest of all stock type linkages to use in a swap. Boats and some race cars (primarily off-road race cars) often employ a hydraulic link between pedal and carb. This is expensive and normally unnecessary for an engine swap.

The best type of linkage to use in an engine swap is the one requiring the least amount of work in order to produce a satisfactory operating mechanism. When installing a late model engine in an early car, many enthusiasts want to retain the older throttle linkage strictly for aesthetic reasons. If you are after stock looks, proceed with care and make sure you know just what needs to be done before cutting and bending or relocating a bell crank bracket on the firewall. Welding rod is easy to bend and can easily be used as a template when designing or reworking part of an existing accelerator-to-throttle link. A template for a bell crank can be cut from tin with snips and used in conjunction with the bent welding rod to completely fabricate a prototype linkage arrangement. This allows you to snip and bend and rework until you are satisfied with the results without having to butcher "real hardware" in an attempt to get it right.

Any time any of this "rod and bellcrank" linkage must be bent or reworked there is a problem with some part of the linkage binding during part of the travel. This can be very unfunny when you have your foot to the firewall in second gear and the bind locks the throttle in the wide open position. Keep this in mind and check the linkage for bind as you are modifying and constructing. Never, ever, attempt to overcome a bind in the linkage by

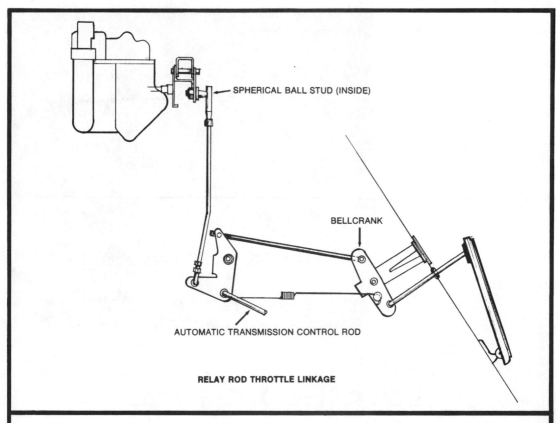

SPHERICAL BALL STUD (INSIDE)

BELLCRANK

AUTOMATIC TRANSMISSION CONTROL ROD

RELAY ROD THROTTLE LINKAGE

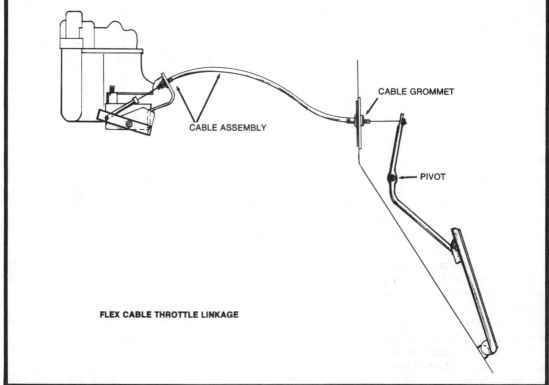

CABLE GROMMET

CABLE ASSEMBLY

PIVOT

FLEX CABLE THROTTLE LINKAGE

Although this looks like a nightmare, all of this is stock Jaguar linkage except the last rod running to the carb. This is a good example of a factory going to a lot of trouble to solve a simple problem.

If any part of the linkage must be bent, do so with care. Small metal parts are easy to fracture.

By now all of this talk about fabricating and bending this and that is probably getting to you. We can understand. In 99% of all modern day swaps the simple solution to throttle linkage problems is with sheathed cable. Late model Ford, GM and Chrysler built cars and trucks—in addition to a great majority of foreign cars and trucks—now use a sheathed cable arrangement for throttle linkage. The pedal arm is part of a bell crank arrangement that bolts to the inside of the firewall. The pedal is at one end of the bellcrank and the cable is attached to the other. The cable is routed through the firewall and forward to the carb. Problems of binding, misalignment and ratios of travel distance are solved instantly by simply bolting in a low cost, factory engineered item.

Hydraulic throttle linkage mentioned earlier can solve a lot of fabricating problems—but it is very expensive when compared to the cable controls and it does not give the "mechanical feel" back to the driver as does other types of

adding more throttle return spring. Work on the linkage until it doesn't bind—period.

Another disadvantage to the older type of linkage is when welding near the firewall to modify the linkage it is easy to start a smouldering fire in the firewall insulation or to burn the insulation off wiring on the opposite side of the firewall. The complications and grief this can cause are practically endless—so keep in mind before lighting the torch.

If any part of the linkage must be bent severly, keep in mind that part is now open to the possibility of material fracture. If you create a hairline crack in the metal when bending it, the crack can only get worse—not better.

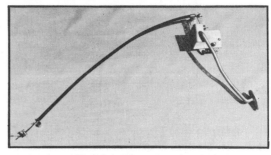

This is an aftermarket universal throttle control assembly designed to be bolted to the inside firewall. This can solve a lot of problems in a hurry.

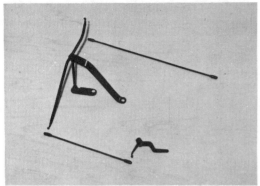

Very early mechanical linkage such as this is difficult to work with and easy to break. If it is to be retained and modified, work with care. Reproduction linkage is often difficult to locate.

When working with this style linkage, make sure it does not bind or go over center when nearing the wide open throttle position. Get this taken care of BEFORE backing out of the garage.

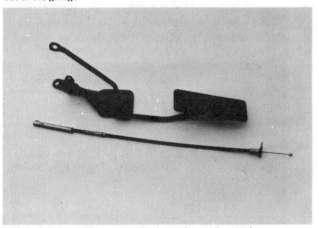

This is a late GM cable setup which attaches to the inside of the firewall and works without modification in most all swaps.

linkage. However, don't rule hydraulic linkage out if you perform a swap in which cable linkage is undesirable from a construction standpoint or from a functional standpoint. In this last area of concern, I am thinking primarily of off-road race cars which might encounter problems with dirt jamming cables in their sheathing.

Anytime mechanical linkage or cable is used to actuate a throttle in an engine swap, it is very important to make sure the finished product does not "overcenter". If the linkage gets pulled or pushed beyond its center point, the linkage will lock. In most cases this occurs as the throttle is nearing the wide open setting which makes for a very dangerous situation. To "slow down" the ratio, the rod or cable end of the bellcrank should be shortened. To "speed up" the ratio the rod or cable end of the bellcrank can be lengthened. There are some real head-scratching formulas for figuring out ratios, but they are so involved that most backyard engine swappers can solve the problem through trial and error faster than they can do all of the math.

Like the rest of an engine swap, throttle linkage should be constructed by the very best method you know how the first time. Putting up with "an almost right" situation and then trying to modify it when you are disgusted, is a problem just looking for a place to crash.

Shifter Linkage

Assuming you are installing a different engine and transmission in the vehicle of your choice, then something will have to be done to effect a gear change in the new transmission—whether it be automatic or stick. In both cases the solutions are fairly obvious, but the choices are many. Since I strongly suggest using an automatic transmission in most all swaps, let's start with the automatics in order to take a closer look at the shift linkage. If a late engine and transmission is being installed in an early car, a late steering column can be installed and column shift for the automatic be effected by modifying a rod running from transmission to the bottom of the new steering column. This updates the interior—which is not always desired and it can create problems in attempting to graft the new column to the old steering box. In most cases, the simple way to solve the problem is use a floor mounted shifter.

Floor mounted shifters can be factory items or aftermarket pieces. In most cases, a wrecking yard unit will be far less expensive than an aftermarket shifter—but not always. Factory shifters are normally designed for one chassis and can be difficult to mount to the floor of an earlier car without extensive rework of the transmission tunnel. The

This is a Jaguar shift unit being used with a Turbo 350 installed in the Jag. This is a rare case of the stock shifter being readily adaptable to the new transmission.

Stock shifting mechanism often works out quite well in an engine swap. The most common problem is often in mounting.

B&M builds this universal type shifter which works out slick for all popular automatic transmissions. This early Plymouth is now powered by a big block Chrysler.

hassle some of these shifters create when being installed makes them a bad buy. Each shifter and each chassis are somewhat different, so take a look before laying down the long green for a wrecking yard shifter you cannot use.

Several companies manufacture floor mounted shifters which are designed for engine swapping and competition use—Hurst and B&M are two brand names that come to mind. In the case of Hurst, a wide variety of shifter handles are offered in an effort to put the shift lever where you want it and in some cases to clear the leading edge of the seat.

If you are the he-man, I'll-make-it-work type, we want to wish you a lot of luck if you try to make a Ford or Chrysler wrecking yard shifter work with a GM transmission. Once again, the plan is to solve

This is a Hurst shifter attached to a GM transmission which is installed in an early Ford frame. Body has been lifted off and set back to facilitate work. Forward end of the X-member is all new to allow the installation of the late powertrain.

the shifter problem in the most practical manner possible—which normally equates to the least amount of work and least amount of money going out the door.

Everything we've said about shift linkage for an automatic transmission goes for stick shifts—but in the case of the stick, problem solving becomes more difficult. All sorts of levers and rods are used

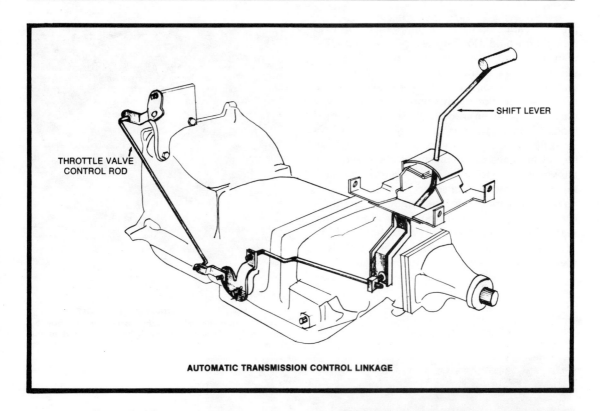

THROTTLE VALVE
CONTROL ROD

SHIFT LEVER

AUTOMATIC TRANSMISSION CONTROL LINKAGE

to transmit motion in various directions from shifter to transmission. In automatic shifters a heavy, sheathed cable is often used for gear selection, but in stick shift transmissions, the cutting, bending and fabricating necessary to adapt this to that gets out of hand in a hurry. Here again, the floor shifter is the easy way out. There are excellent factory and aftermarket shifters available for most three and four speed transmissions. Just make sure you buy the right shifter for the transmission you plan to install.

This last point should not be passed over lightly. If you buy a small block Chevy and four speed transmission in a wrecking yard you could wind up with a Chevrolet, Muncie, Saginaw or Borg Warner transmission. The same holds true for a three speed stick shift. The problem of different manufacturers making transmissions for one line of cars does not end there—each manufacturer may have more than one four speed or three speed. For instance, there are five different Borg Warner three speeds. It is for this reason we include the complete Hurst transmission identification chart for three and four speed stick shift and automatics.

Any linkage encountered in an engine swap will most likely be a nit-picking, time consuming

This is a low cost, aftermarket shifter attached to a Powerglide transmission. The vehicle is a Datsun truck. That is a pretty good size hole to cover.

problem eating up far more hours than you ever thought it would. Don't make work for yourself— plan ahead and do what is practical for you before you are so deep in the problem the solution is not practical for anyone. If all of this sounds like the obvious—it is. But try this one on for size. How much of a problem would it be to install a small block Chevy and a four speed transmission in a late Chevy van which currently is running a small block Chevy and a column shift three speed? The answer is: next to impossible. There is no such thing as a domestic four speed stick shift column. To fabricate a mechanical floor mounted shifter is extremely difficult and it would take more money than the finished product would be worth to figure out how to cable shift a stick shift four speed. Look before you leap—be practical.

This is a Hurst dual gate shifter being installed in small car being outfitted with a big engine. A console will now be fabricated and carpeted to hide the bottom part of the shifter.

Several firms build fiberglass shifter tunnels such as this which can often be used when a transmission is swapped.

The following six pages contain transmission identifications for four speed, three speed and automatic transmissions found in virtually every American automobile. We thank Hurst for supplying these.

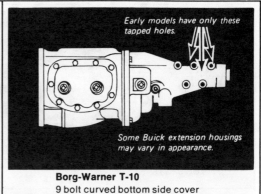

Borg-Warner T-10
9 bolt curved bottom side cover

Early models have only these tapped holes.

Some Buick extension housings may vary in appearance.

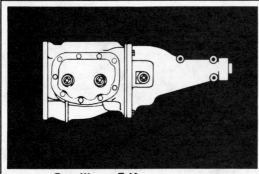

Borg-Warner T-10
9 bolt curved bottom side cover

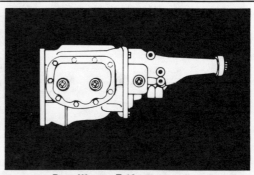

Borg-Warner T-10
9 bolt curved bottom side cover

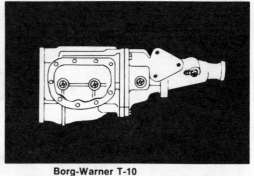

Borg-Warner T-10
9 bolt curved bottom side cover

Borg-Warner T-10
9 bolt curved bottom side cover

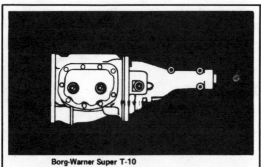

Borg-Warner Super T-10
9 bolt curved bottom side cover

New Process
10 bolt side cover

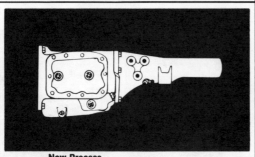

New Process
10 bolt side cover

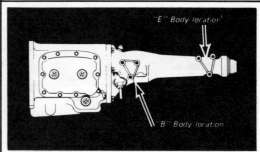

"E" Body location

"B" Body location

New Process
10 bolt side cover

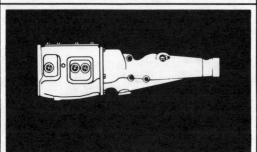

Ford T & C
10 bolt top cover

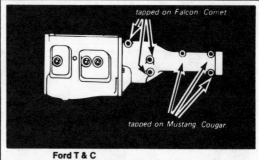

tapped on Falcon, Comet

tapped on Mustang, Cougar

Ford T & C
10 bolt top cover

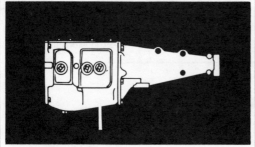

Ford T & C
10 bolt top cover

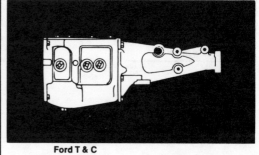

Ford T & C
10 bolt top cover

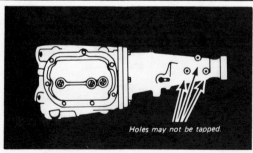

Saginaw
7 bolt side cover

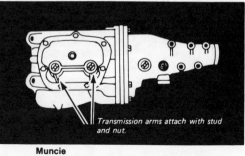

Muncie
7 bolt side cover used from 1963-68

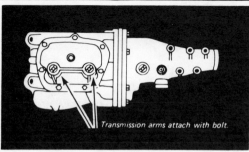

Muncie
7 bolt side cover 1969 and later

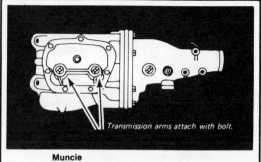

Muncie
7 bolt side cover 1970, 454 Chevelle

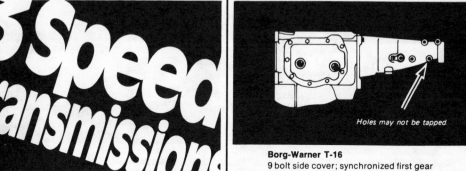

Borg-Warner T-16
9 bolt side cover; synchronized first gear

Borg-Warner T-85
9 bolt curved bottom side cover

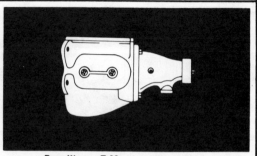

Borg-Warner T-86
6 bolt top cover

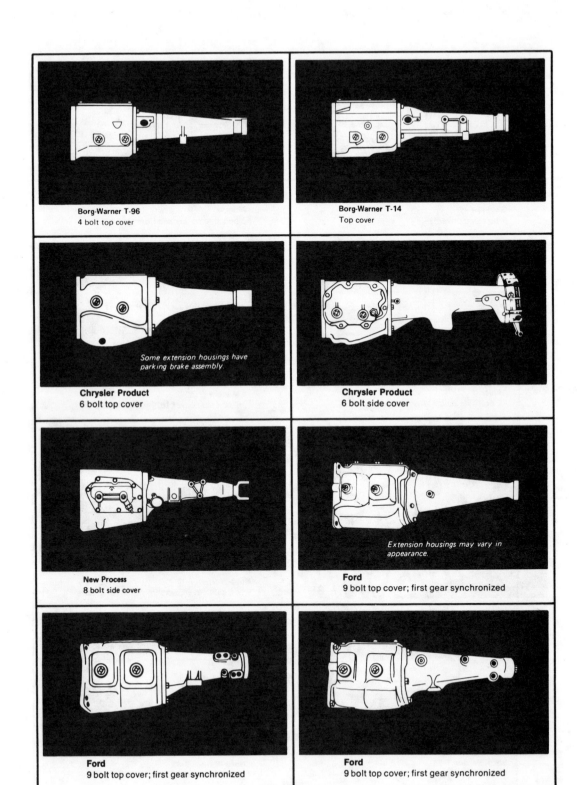

Borg-Warner T-96
4 bolt top cover

Borg-Warner T-14
Top cover

Chrysler Product
6 bolt top cover

*Some extension housings have
parking brake assembly.*

Chrysler Product
6 bolt side cover

New Process
8 bolt side cover

Ford
9 bolt top cover; first gear synchronized

*Extension housings may vary in
appearance.*

Ford
9 bolt top cover; first gear synchronized

Ford
9 bolt top cover; first gear synchronized

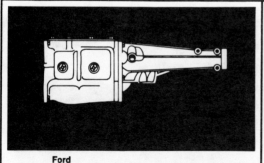

Ford
9 bolt top cover; first gear synchronized

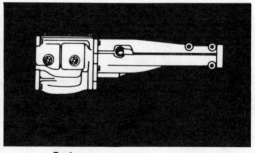

Ford
4 or 6 bolt top cover; first gear not synchronized

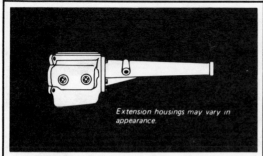

Extension housings may vary in appearance.

Ford
6 bolt top cover; first gear not synchronized

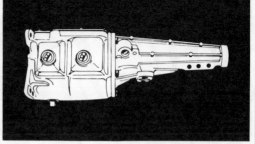

Ford
9 bolt top cover; first gear synchronized

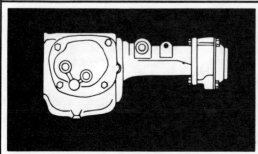

Chevrolet
4 bolt side cover with torque-tube drive

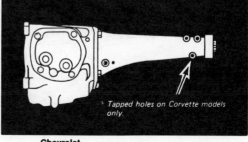

Tapped holes on Corvette models only.

Chevrolet
4 bolt side cover with round gear selector shafts

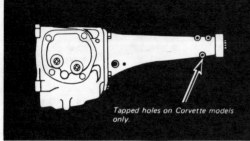

Tapped holes on Corvette models only.

Chevrolet
4 bolt side cover with keyed selector shaft

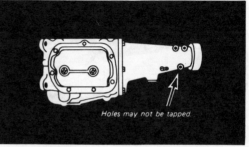

Holes may not be tapped.

Saginaw
7 bolt side cover; first gear synchronized
CAUTION: This transmission closely resembles 351 Muncie.

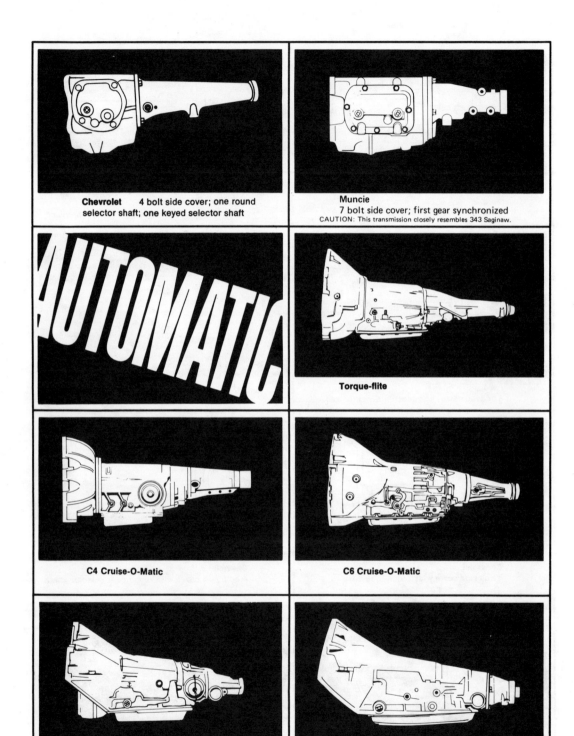

Chevrolet   4 bolt side cover; one round selector shaft; one keyed selector shaft

Muncie
7 bolt side cover; first gear synchronized
CAUTION: This transmission closely resembles 343 Saginaw.

Torque-flite

C4 Cruise-O-Matic

C6 Cruise-O-Matic

350 Turbo Hydra-matic

400 Turbo Hydra-matic

Electrical Considerations
of Swapping

What to do about wiring in engine swaps causes a lot of unnecessary grief. Had we been writing this book twenty years ago, we would have gone through a long exercise of outlining at least three ways of wiring a 12-volt engine being installed in a 6-volt car—right down to telling you how to take a 6-volt tap off a 12-volt battery. Fortunately, things are done differently these days. Of the several hundred engine swaps I've seen in the past five years, I have yet to see one retaining part of a 6-volt system in an otherwise 12-volt car. For the time being let's not muddy the water with a long, rambling discussion of amps and resistance. If you are installing a 12-volt engine in a 6-volt car, simply change all light bulbs to 12-volt units and use a Stewart Warner resistor #41212036 for each electrically actuated instrument. Before getting started you should know that voltage dropping devices never work just like you would like for them to on radios and heaters. The solution here is to install a 12-volt radio and a 12-volt motor in the heater. Six-volt wiring is more than adequate for a 12-volt system—complete rewiring is unnecessary.

I asked engine swapping professional Andy Herbert the most common mistake an amateur makes in engine swap wiring. His reply was that most guys get off on the wrong foot immediately by buying an engine without an alternator or generator. This leads to all sorts of discouraging,

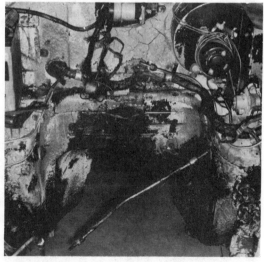

Although this firewall is pretty clean, the wiring is in sad shape due to little or no thought as to what goes where when the engine was removed. This will mean slow going when the new engine is in place. Small tags or masking tape can be used to label the ends of wires.

This wiring is brittle, frayed and is bound to cause problems—with or without an engine swap. The plan is to replace all of it instead of trying to patch in to the decaying system with new wire here and there.

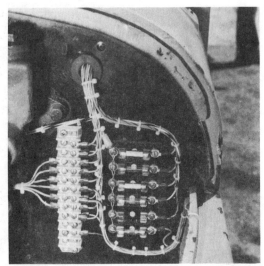

Terminal strips and fuse blocks are available at automotive parts stores and when complete rewiring is necessary, both items can save a lot of time and make for a very neat job.

This neat wiring job was done when a big block Chevy was installed in an early Buick. Note how straightforward and simple the job appears.

time consuming attempts to fabricate mounting brackets and find alternators or generators at decent prices in working condition. As we point out elsewhere in this book, the plan is to buy the engine complete—with alternator or generator and all of the brackets intact. In the long run, this saves time and money. The second mistake in the electrical department on an engine swap is to attempt to wire the engine compartment without a wiring diagram for the engine, which shows a separate wiring diagram for the engine and generating source.

The great majority of all engine swapping done today involves an engine wired for 12-volts with an alternator as the source for electrical power. Most of the vehicles involved in the swaps of today were originally wired for 12-volt systems—

Here's a good example of bad wiring in an engine swap. Some new wiring was patched into old wiring and the routing of the wire allows it to move, chafe and eventually cause grief.

If you are really concerned about appearances under the hood, most all of the wiring can be hidden under the dash—as is the case with this truck. Unfortunately, wiring under the dash can often be a bear t work on. Keep it in mind.

The terminals on alternators are clearly marked, but sometimes the markings are abbreviations or numbers. Our wiring diagrams clear this up.

but probably one half of those which undergo an engine transplant started life with a generator under the hood. Thus, most of the questions concerning engine swap wiring center around converting from generator to alternator as a power source.

Let's say the car in question is a '55 Chevy—12-volt with a generator. The new engine being bolted in is a big block Chevy—12-volt with an alternator. What's the plan? Use the regulator that goes with the alternator and follow the diagram shown on these pages that relates to GM wiring. There is one small catch here and you should be aware of it before plunging ahead. Use the regulator intended to be used with the alternator you have—not just a 12-volt alternator regulator for a GM product. The regulator must be matched with the output of the alternator. Determining which regulator to buy is actually pretty simple. Somewhere on the alternator you'll find a tag with a bunch of numbers stamped on it—or there will be numbers stamped directly on the case of the alternator. We have a Delco-Remy alternator on an Olds engine which bears the number 1100700-55A. This is stamped on the front section of the case. Under this is stamped 4L10-12v NEG. This means the alternator is 12 volt negative ground and is rated at 55 amps. It also means that with all of these numbers, the man behind the parts counter can supply you with the correct regulator. If you can buy the regulator that goes with the engine at the time of purchasing the engine—so

Electrical tape, wire clamps and tie wraps are all used here to secure the alternator wiring to the inner fender panel. Nice.

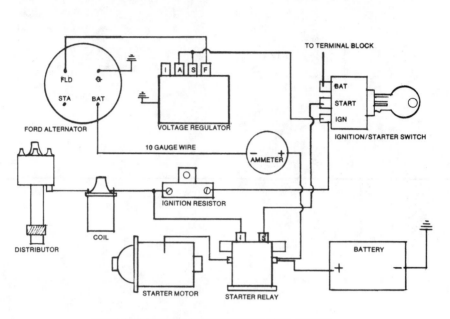

FORD ALTERNATOR IGNITION/CHARGING CIRCUIT

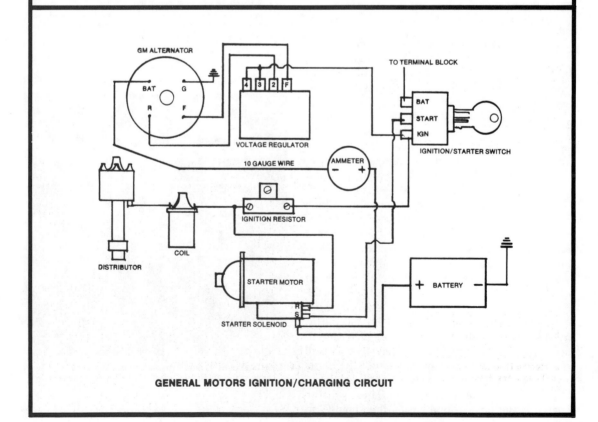

GENERAL MOTORS IGNITION/CHARGING CIRCUIT

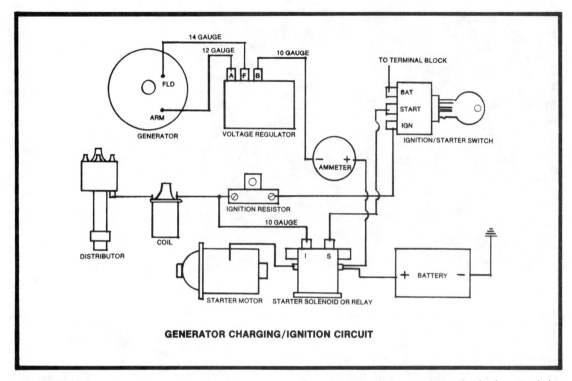

14 GAUGE
12 GAUGE
10 GAUGE

FLD

ARM

GENERATOR

A F B

VOLTAGE REGULATOR

TO TERMINAL BLOCK

BAT

START

IGN

IGNITION/STARTER SWITCH

AMMETER

IGNITION RESISTOR

10 GAUGE

DISTRIBUTOR

COIL

STARTER MOTOR   STARTER SOLENOID OR RELAY

I   S

+ BATTERY −

GENERATOR CHARGING/IGNITION CIRCUIT

much the better. If not, I'd advise going to a parts counter and getting a new one.

Use the regulator that goes with the alternator —even if you put a GM alternator on a Ford engine—use the regulator matched to that particular alternator. Are there any exceptions? No. Occassionally, you'll run across an "odd ball" but the rule still stands. For example, most Ford engines are equipped with Ford-built alternators and regulators. But some of the time, the larger, more heavily equipped cars will be found using an

alternator/regulator package built for Ford by Leece Neville. A Ford regulator designed for a 42 amp Ford alternator will not work on a 42 amp Leece Neville alternator. In this case, you'll even find a different number of terminals on the alternators and regulators.

Take a look at the voltage regulators in the wiring diagrams offered for GM, Ford and Chrysler built cars. Note that all of the regulators are different. Hopefully, this will serve to reinforce what we've already said about using the regulator

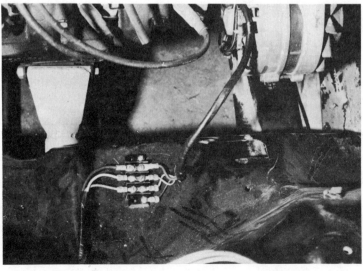

Wiring need not be elaborate or fancy to be effective. This terminal block was already in place on the inner fender panel and the new alternator wiring was simply connected to it so the current will flow to the new regulator mounted on the firewall.

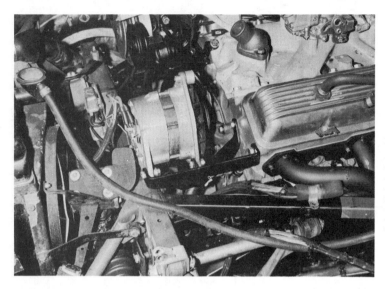

Just in case you are ever faced with the problem—it's nice to know an alternator can be turned in either direction and still produce current. Andy Herbert came up with this arrangement when he installed a small block Chevy in a Jaguar—one of the most time consuming, difficult swaps we have ever encountered.

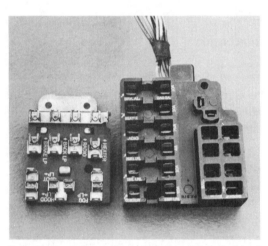

Early GM products use the fuse block on the left which is simple to work with in most any engine swap. The later style GM block makes for an unsanitary job because the existing wiring going into the block must be retained.

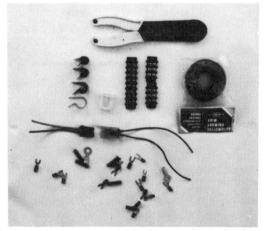

There is a wide variety of low cost automotive wiring hardware which can be used to solve any problem you can think of when working on new or old wiring. Local parts stores have a wide variety of wiring tools and hardware.

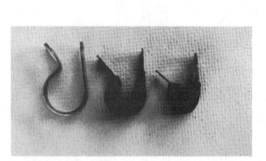

Automotive parts stores have all sorts of wire hold-down devices which should be used liberally to keep the wiring bundles where they belong.

that was designed to work with the alternator. Regulators contain relays—and alternator regulators usually have only one or two relays compared to the three relays used with most generators. With an alternator system, one relay is a field relay, the other is a voltage limiter. The field relay connects the rotor's field windings to the battery as soon as the ignition switch is turned on. The output of an alternator is self current limiting so there is no need for a current limiting relay just as there is no need for a cutout relay in the secondary circuit. Chrysler has now designed their system with only one relay in the regulator—it simply limits voltage.

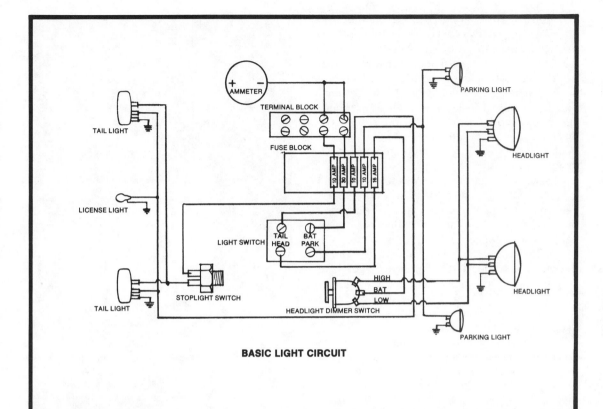

BASIC LIGHT CIRCUIT

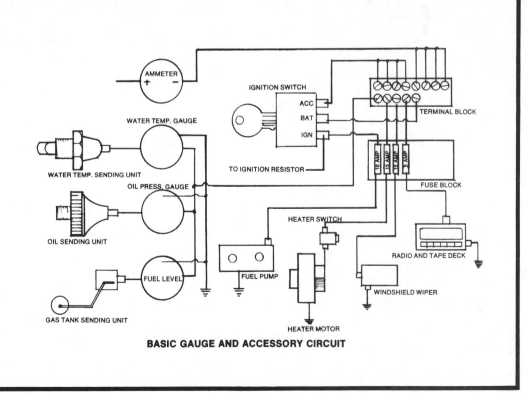

BASIC GAUGE AND ACCESSORY CIRCUIT

If you have this book propped on the work bench where you also have a dirty alternator and not so dirty regulator you'll probably discover that the terminals on the alternator are clearly marked, while the terminals on the regulator lead to some head-scratching. Depending on the make you'll find STA (stator), BAT (battery), GRD (ground), FLD (field) and R (relay) on the alternator. Over on the regulator you are liable to find terminals marked F, 2, 3, 4. This is very common on GM charging systems.

Ground the regulator and the alternator. The F on the alternator connects to F on the regulator. Terminal R connects to terminal 2. The terminal marked BAT on the alternator connects to terminal 3 on the regulator and also to the battery side of the ignition switch. The number 4 terminal on the regulator connects to the "no charge" lamp and then to the ignition side of the ignition switch. The ACC terminal on the ignition switch then runs to the other side of the "no charge" lamp to complete the circuit.

An increasing number of alternators have integral regulators—in other words, there is no regulator "box" to mount on the firewall or fender panel. This makes it even easier, since in effect the factory has already wired the alternator to the regulator for you. The terminals on the back of the alternator now get connected to the existing vehicle wiring that did go to the old regulator. None of the lighting or instrument wiring need be changed.

If the vehicle is quite old or the wiring is botched up and in bad shape with corroded terminals and wire with cracked insulation, you'll most likely be ahead of the game by completely rewiring that portion relating to charging, starting and instrumentation. Simply follow the diagram that relates to the alternator being used.

Fortunately, the days of the voltage dropping device are just about dead. There are several versions of this device.

Driveshaft Problems

Chances are very good if you swap engines in a late model car or truck that you will need to have a driveshaft built specifically for the swap. This is routinely easy to have done once you know how to go about it. Here is the simple way to go about it. Let's assume for the sake of telling you the easy-way-to-go-about-it that you are installing a small block Chevy with a PowerGlide in a '54 Ford pickup. Just before the Ford engine threw a rod through the side of the block, the rear axle assembly started to howl; so you rightfully assume it needs to be replaced in the course of the engine swap. After shopping around for rear axle assem-blies you learn that a Javelin rear axle is the correct width (outer drum to outer drum) and since there is little call for this item at the local wrecking yard, you can get one in the gear ratio you want for $50.00 less than a Ford or Chevy rear axle. You install the rear axle and the new engine and transmission. In a case like this, what do you do about a driveshaft? The same think you would do in any other engine/trans or rear axle swap.

Here's the plan. When you go to the wrecking yard to take delivery of the engine/trans or of the rear axle assembly for your dreamboat, get the drive shaft. If you are changing engine/trans and

When measuring a driveshaft for correct length, measure from yoke center to yoke center—and just to make sure there is no misunderstanding, tell the machinist that's the way you measured it.

The difference in output shaft splines shown here is the reason you buy the driveshaft that goes with the transmission when you buy an engine and transmission for a swap. Sure saves some money and a lot of running around.

rear axle you could wind up with three driveshafts —one that goes with the new transmission, one that goes with the new rear axle and one that came in the car when you bought it. Fine. It is easier to throw a driveshaft or two away after you get the vehicle running than it is to scrounge what you need when it isn't running. Let's go back over this plan: when you buy an engine/trans combination for a swap, get the drive shaft. If you buy a different rear axle assembly, get the driveshaft that mated with the axle. Doing this will insure you have all hardware needed to get the one driveshaft you need to bridge the gap between transmission A and rear axle B in vehicle C.

Driveshafts are used in cars, trucks, back hoes, corn binders, combines, streetsweepers, ditch diggers and stationary industrial equipment—just to name a few of the applications. As a consequence, driveshafts are around in an infinite variety of lengths and with a great variety of diameters, yokes and splines. The combinations are practically endless.

One of the last and least things you need to worry about in an engine swap is the driveshaft. Regardless of what you are swapping into what, plan on having a custom made driveshaft. It is really quite simple. Install the engine and transmission and new rear axle if that is part of the swap. After making sure the driveline is phased (which has already been explained), slide under the car and bolt the driveshaft that goes with the rear axle to the companion flange attached to the nose of the pinion gear. Just let the forward end of this driveshaft rest on the garage floor. Now take the driveshaft that goes with the transmission and shove the forward end of it into the rear of the transmission. Shove it in until it won't go any further—then pull it back out exactly ¾-inch. At this point you will probably need a helping hand. The center to center distance between front and rear U-joint cross now needs to be measured with a steel tape. Make sure the tape is tight, make sure the vehicle weight is resting on all four wheels, and make sure the measurement is from center to center on the front and rear U-joint cross. If you can call it that—the hard part is now over. The procedure now is to use a piece of chalk to mark the front driveshaft, the rear driveshaft and the center to center length of the driveshaft you need to finish the job. A machine shop can now do the rest.

Driveshafts are everyday jobs for machine shops all over the country. The machinist in a city might do a lot of truck work, the machinist in the suburbs might do a lot of industrial work, and the one man shop in a farming community might specialize in farm equipment, but when you boil it all down, a driveshaft is a driveshaft. If a machinist cannot handle the job for you, it will most likely be because he does not have a lathe of sufficient size. If that is the case, he'll be glad to recommend a competent shop. When I lived in a town too small to have a machine shop, I've gone so far as to make arrangements by phone with a machine shop in a neighboring town for "rush service" which allowed me to drive over with the driveshaft, drop it off, take in a movie and then pick up the completed driveshaft a couple of hours later.

DRIVESHAFT BALANCE

Like any rotating part, a driveshaft is subject to vibrations and harmonics which are amplified by imbalance. Driveshafts are balanced as they are built. The balance of the shaft may or may not be affected when the shaft is modified, but I would

Some passenger car driveshafts have an inner and outer tube with rubber sandwiched in between for a distance. This soaks up minor vibrations and noise. When cutting a shaft like this, specify that the rubber be left intact.

suggest having it balanced at the time it is cut. Some machine shops can balance a shaft and some can't—but those that do not have the equipment can invariably tell you where it can be balanced. If you are smoking this out of the yellow pages, look under "balancing" or "machine

shops". A driveshaft that is not balanced will make strange sounds and sometimes weird vibrations. This may occur at any speed or at all speeds. If the driveshaft is balanced and the weird happenings continue, the next place to look for trouble is improper driveline phasing.

DRIVESHAFT PARTS

If for some reason you need any part of a driveshaft assembly to aid the machinist in the construction of a special driveshaft, you need only to check with a large auto parts firm. TRW, Spicer and Borg Warner all have catalogs devoted to driveshaft hardware. From these catalogs you can obtain everything needed to construct a driveshaft—including the tubing.

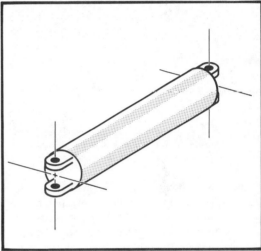

A machinist will know that the pivot points of each yoke must parallel when putting the shaft back together—which is something for you to keep in mind if you ever attempt to build a driveshaft.

Four wheel drive driveshaft angularity need not be severe—as shown in this Herbert and Meeks swap of a Chevy in a Toyota Landcruiser.

This has to be the worst driveshaft angle I've ever seen, but the swap was a success since the small block Chevy in the early Jeep was used for four wheel drive, low speed work in the boondocks.

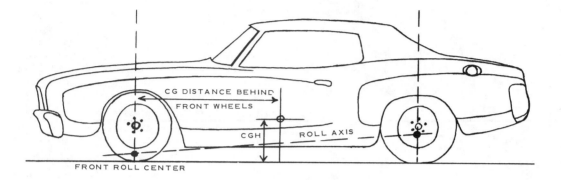

CG DISTANCE BEHIND
FRONT WHEELS

CGH ROLL AXIS

FRONT ROLL CENTER

Suspension and Steering

Suspension and steering problems almost never crop up in a swap if the entire swap has been thought out in advance. Anyone taking the time to make an assessment of the steering and suspension situation most likely won't go through with a swap that will create problems in this area. Let's

consider the problems individually—find out how problems can arise, how to avoid them, and how to cure them.

In putting a full-size engine in a compact—such as a full size V8 in a Pinto or Vega, the new engine and transmission will add roughly 200 pounds to

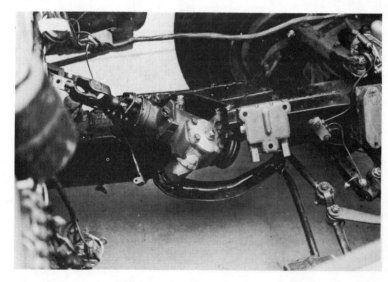

This is a late GM power steering box installed in a Rolls Royce about to be outfitted with a small block Chevy! Note the extensive work done to the frame to provide clearance for the engine. Note also the heavy reinforcing done to the fabricated steering arm.

Olds Toronado steering shaft will yield this beefy U-joint—a very popular item to be used in solving steering problems in swaps.

Note that this power steering box is mounted to the outside of the frame rail and ahead of the axle in order to maintain the integrity of the stock steering system.

the front suspension. Since this weight is all "spring weight", it means an extra load is being carried by the front springs. The net effect will be having a car with softer than stock front suspension. The front end will feel mushy and the front of the car will be somewhat lower than it was with the stock engine. The springs will reach their limit of travel sooner with the additional weight, which means the front suspension will bottom out on less of a bump than with the stock engine. There are a couple of things which can be done to remedy these maladies. Fortunately, neither are very expensive or time consuming nor do they require a great deal of skill.

The first step in making a front suspension stiffer is to install stiffer springs. These are readily available. The stiffest springs are not made by the car manufacturers but by replacement parts manufacturers. In other words, if you want stiffer springs for a Vega, don't start your shopping at the Chevy dealership—but at the local independent parts house. Those firms which manufacture aftermarket springs—firms like TRW and Moog—generally make them about 20% stiffer than similar factory items. So in shopping for replacement springs which are stiffer than stock, belly up to an independent parts counter. At this point you should know station wagon springs are stiffer than passenger car springs for the same basic vehicle and front springs for air conditioned vehicles are stiffer than those meant to be installed on non-air conditioned vehicles. Thus, if you have installed a

Even the factories have problems. Jaguar sedan has two U-joints in the steering shaft in order to get everything where they wanted it.

pickup trucks having leaf springs, the simple thing to do is to add more leaves to the front spring assemblies. Leaf springs can also be re-arched by spring specialty firms. This has the effect of raising the vehicle and making the springs slightly stiffer —but very slightly.

Stiffer front (and rear) springs for full size domestic cars are often carried by the manufacturer's dealer (Chevy, Ford, etc.) under the guise of heavy duty, police or taxi options.

The second route to take in increasing the stiffness of the front suspension is to install air bag devices in the coil springs. This is obviously limited to those vehicles equipped with coil springs in the front suspension. This is also limited to those vehicles which have the shock absorbers mounted on the outside of the coils. Air bags are very tough rubber bladders which are placed on the inside of the coil and then inflated with a slight amount (7-12 lbs.) of air pressure. This has the net effect of making the springs stiffer.

Once you have added extra weight to the front end in the form of a heavier engine, and then stiffened the front springs, you may find you have a handling problem with the vehicle. This is particularly so if you drive the car "vigorously." The addition of more weight at the front, and the addition of stiffer springs at the front, will disrupt the car's balance of roll resistance between the

Swapping steering columns is becoming increasingly popular. Normally some provision will have to be made for anchoring the column in the floor or firewall and at the dash. This is a simple fabricated piece that gets the job done.

small block Chevy V8 in a '74 Vega coupe, you can ask for Moog or TRW front springs for a '74 air-conditioned Vega station wagon. In the case of MoPar or some foreign vehicles using torsion bar front suspension, the same basic rule of replacement parts applies with the added bonus of being able to adjust the torsion bars upon installation to make the front of the car sit higher or lower. To increase the front suspension stiffness of older

front end and the rear end. In effect, what you will find is that the car will understeer or push. For example, say you drive particularly hard into a turn. With an understeer condition, the front end of the vehicle will want to go straight, and you will have to apply more and more steering wheel lock to correct, if you can correct it at all before you bounce off a curb or wall.

The remedy for the understeer condition you

Here's another approach to the steering column swap. A muffler clamp is used in conjunction with a piece of angle iron. In the finished car this will all be covered with carpet.

Never compromise when anchoring anything having to do with the steering system.

This is a Saginaw manual steering box mounted on the inside of a frame rail. Note the close proximity of the new clutch cross shaft to the steering column.

have built in is simple. It can be balanced by stiffening the roll resistance at the rear end of the car. If the car is not equipped with a rear anti-roll bar (or stabilizer bar), add one. If it has one, go to a stiffer one. If you do not want to add an anti-roll bar in the rear, you can achieve the same effect by stiffening the left rear and right rear springs. Follow the same procedure for choosing stiffer rear springs as outlined for the front springs.

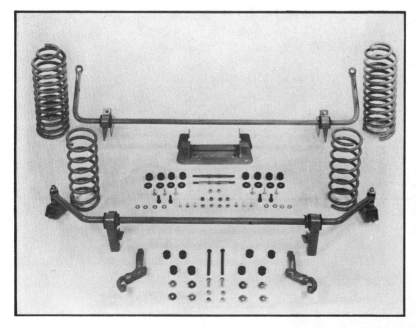

Some engine swap kits such as those designed to put a small block Chevy in the back seat of a Corvair have optional suspension packages designed just for the swap. This makes a very potent package.

Completely re-engineering the suspension system of a car is best left to an expert. Here, a complete Jaguar suspension system has been installed in an early Ford frame. This takes a complete understanding of suspension geometry to pull off correctly.

STEERING SYSTEM

No where is the engine swapper more liable to encounter serious trouble than when modifying a steering system in order to accomodate a different engine. It is true that a worm and sector steering gear box can be moved from the inside of a frame rail to the outside; that a rack and pinion gear can be used in place of a worm and sector box and that a hundred other modifications can be made to accomodate an engine. Like the engine swap itself—the possibilities are endless.

All of the questions concerning modifications to steering gear should be countered with your honest appraisal of what is practical for you. A rather complete understanding of steering systems is necessary before modifying any part of the system. If any fabrication or welding is necessary, then it should be of the highest quality. Since it is impossible to anticipate all of the questions which might arise in this area, we suggest you consult a front end alignment shop or frame rebuilding firm in order to get some qualified comments on the feasibility and practicality of what you have in mind. A frame rebuilding firm or a qualified welder should be able to take care of any fabrication needed.

As with an engine swap, you will save time, money and a lot of headaches if all steering modifications are thought out before being executed.

Do not—under any circumstances—attempt to modify a steering system for a street driven vehicle based on a system being used on a drag race car. Although adequate for drag racing, the steering system will most likely be far too weak to use on a daily basis on city streets. Fortunately, technical inspectors employed by racing associations do an excellent job of scrutinizing modifications made to steering and suspension components on race cars.

Here again, a muffler clamp is used to anchor a new steering column to an older dash. There should always be a brace running from the bottom of the dash forward to the firewall to provide stiffness to the structure.

A little ingenuity (and some hammer work) prevent having to build special headers to solve this clearance problem between spark plug and steering shaft.

Four Wheel Drive Conversions

Quite aside from racing, off-roaders are real performance buffs. They tinker, they tune and they swap engines and gearboxes like no other group of automotive enthusiasts. Jeep and Toyota hoods are being slammed on everything from Pinto four bangers to Cadillacs. Engine-swapped four wheel drive vehicles are very popular dual purpose toys. Since the early 1970's a number of

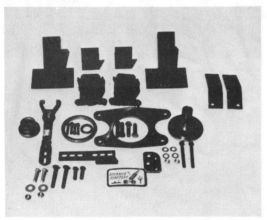

Several firms—such as Advance Adapters—sell complete kits with everything needed to perform a certain swap. For most swappers this saves time and money in the long run.

shops have come into business specializing in four wheel drive swaps—but the vast majority of swaps are being done by guys at home in their garage with a friend or neighbor giving assistance and a patient wife providing the coffee.

Most off-roaders want to be able to cruise at freeway speed in their rigs (oft times towing a loaded trailer) and still retain the capability of crawling around in the rocks and sand at a snail's pace. The bewildering complexity of all those shift levers sprouting from the floor of an early vehicle demand dedication and many an off-roader opts for an easier to drive combination of larger engine, automatic transmission and new transfer case. Another vehicle owner happy with the stock engine and transfer case might be stuck with a three speed transmission with a non-synchro first gear. When the choice boils down to selling the vehicle or switching to a four speed box, the possibility of going ahead with an engine and transmission swap often comes into play.

Engine swapping for the off-roader is somewhat more involved than most other swaps because the owner normally wants the vehicle to be entirely adequate for on and off-road use. Somewhere along the line there must be a compromise or two.

World War II vintage vehicles are gaining popularity in the engine swap ranks. Here a large block Mopar is being dropped into an older Dodge four wheel drive truck.

Overlooking this usually results in a four wheel drive that goes up for sale about thirty days after the swap is complete because the completed package did not turn out to be the vehicle the owner dreamed it would.

Everyone seems to have a little different idea about what they want in their "ultimate off-roader" so we can't possibly try to second guess all of you, but just for grins let's construct a hypothetical situation to show how a project can get out of hand in a hurry.

Let's take the case of the young enthusiast who has never owned a four wheel drive vehicle before, but he's been out in the brush several times with friends. The ownership bug bites and the shopping begins. Money is in short supply, so our young friend winds up with an old Jeep equipped with a four cylinder engine, three speed transmission, 4.88 gears in the front and rear axles and stock size tires and wheels. In today's world of off-roading, this is about as plain jane and low cost as they come. Compared to the newer rigs, this one is a real handful to drive because of the archaic gear box and transfer case. Due to the gearing and limitations of the elderly engine, long distance freeway travel is completely ruled out. Obviously, this is a prime candidate for an engine swap. Top speed will be increased by the larger, better breathing engine and the newer transfer

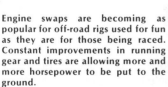

Engine swaps are becoming as popular for off-road rigs used for fun as they are for those being raced. Constant improvements in running gear and tires are allowing more and more horsepower to be put to the ground.

case and automatic will make the Jeep so much easier to drive, that the wife can drive the Jeep to her job and use it for grocery shopping.

Hoosier Machine Products makes a complete kit for installing a small block Chevy into early Jeep vehicles — in this case a four wheel drive station wagon.

Installing a small block Chevy into a Toyota Landcruiser is perhaps the most popular four wheel drive engine swap going. This is a Herbert installation.

At this point some folding green paper changes hands. A small block Chevy, 350 Turbo and late model transfer case are hauled home and the swap begins. Engine mounts and some other miscellaneous pieces of hardware are readily available for this swap and our young friend is a pretty fair fabricator so the swap is done in about two weeks of pretty steady spare time work. While the swap is under way an ad in the local paper leads

The Mazda rotary engine is beginning to increase in popularity as more and more appear in wrecking yards. This is a Hoosier Machine conversion of an M38A Jeep.

this novice Jeeper to a very good buy on a set of four high flotation tires mounted on wide rims that bolt right up to the drums on the Jeep in question. In a fever, more cash changes hands and the large wheels and tires get bolted in place. At this point, the wife is probably told something to the effect that the larger tires and wheels are necessary to handle all of the new power and secondly it will allow the Jeep to go anywhere one of the newer and far more expensive rigs will go. Thirty minutes of test driving when the swap is complete reveals several things. In the first place, the Jeep accelerates like it was fired from a gun. Secondly, it will maintain freeway speed and get there in a hurry. Unfortunately, the engine is turning such high RPM at freeway speed that gas mileage has dropped to seven miles per gallon and the noise level has increased over the little four banger. The wife admits the automatic transmission really makes it a lot easier to drive from one stoplight to the next — but what's wrong with the steering? The steering with the stock tires and wheels was stiff for the young lady, but the larger tires and wheels have increased the steering effort to the level of "plenty hard". For her, parallel parking is now out of the question.

Ah yes, says the more experienced four wheeler. Power steering should have been installed to compensate for the greater engine weight and the resistance of the larger tires. The engine speed can be reduced for freeway travel by changing the gear ratio in the axles — or by installing an overdrive in the rear driveline. Both are rather time consuming and more money must change hands.

The point of all of this is not to discourage anyone from installing a small block Chevy in an early Jeep—for there is nothing wrong with the swap per se. The point is that one thing often leads to another and if goals are not clearly defined before starting a swap then good money winds up being thrown after bad in an attempt to solve the individual problems. Take an honest look at the forest—not just each tree as you come to it.

Fortunately for the off-roader contemplating a swap there are literally dozens of kits and scores of individual components available to make the swap easy to complete. Many of the swaps have been done hundreds of times—the ease of installation contributing greatly to their popularity. These are the swaps the novice can have confidence in tackling. A difficult swap in a four wheeler can create some real problems for an experienced swapper. If the manufacturer of engine conversion hardware says you don't want to do a particular swap—take his word for it—he's probably been there before, which is why he doesn't offer the hardware.

A four wheel drive vehicle is a special interest device and although their popularity is increasing, they still appeal to a rather small percentage of the cary buying public. I mention this for a reason. In the world of four wheel drive, a professionally done swap can greatly upgrade the value of an older vehicle. They demand (and get) premium dollar when sold. A botched swap—no matter the quality of the conversion hardware—will leave you with a vehicle no one wants, and especially not you.

In conclusion, I would suggest becoming very, very familiar with off-roading before plunging into a four wheel drive swap.

This Hoosier conversion shows a 389 Pontiac installed in an early Wagoneer. Vehicle is equipped with power steering, power brakes and air conditioning.

A growing number of transmission and transfer case swaps are possible as more and more hardware becomes available from suppliers such as Advance.

Built strictly as a test bed for their own conversion hardware, the Hoosier "Hinny" allows for rapid change of running gear components.

Cost Guide

It can be quite difficult to estimate just how much a swap will cost by the time the car is finally ready to drive. You'll probably want to make an estimate of the job though and that is a wise thing to do. Hopefully, this list will help. Not every item on the list will apply to every swap, but by being on the list they may serve as a gentle reminder something else might crop up—so be prepared to revise your estimate accordingly.

Engine

Allowances for any parts of the engine that are missing - starter, alternator, air cleaner, etc. _____

Transmission_____

Transmission adapter_____

Engine mounts_____

Frame mounts_____

Transmission crossmember_____

Miscellaneous hardware—nuts, bolts, radiator hose, heater hose, etc. _____

Paint for engine and compartment _____

Recharge air conditioning system_____

Chrome plating _____

Driveshaft _____

Driveshaft machining _____

Rear axle _____

Rear axle machining _____

Clutch linkage hardware _____

Radiator _____

Radiator boil out _____

Radiator reworking _____

Headers _____

Exhaust system to the rear of headers or manifolds _____

Suspension upgrading such as new springs, shocks, anti-
   sway bars _____

Special oil pan _____

Remote oil filter _____

Remote oil cooler _____

Shifter hardware _____

Throttle linkage hardware _____

Electric fuel pump _____

Clutch and pressure plate _____

Steam cleaning of new engine _____

Steam cleaning of engine compartment _____

Steering linkage hardware or special modifications _____

Fabrication and welding _____

Wiring hardware _____

Instruments _____

Tool rental _____

Body and paint work necessary such as hood scoop for
   clearance _____

MC 5414933002182484

5/91

Other books from Steve Smith Autosports

Chevy Heavy Duty Parts List

It is up-to-date with all the newest stuff from the factory. Complete with all engine and driveline goodies, plus much more miscellaneous reference info for the racer. Includes all hi performance parts for the V6 Chevy. **#S120 . . . $4.95**

The Complete Karting Guide

The complete guide to kart racing, for every class from beginner to enduro. Contains: Buying a kart and equipment • Setting up a kart — tires, weight distribution, tire readings, plug reading, exhaust tuning, gearing, aerodynamics • Engine care • Competition tips • And more. **#S140 . . . $9.95**

Racing The Yamaha KT 100-S Engine

Hi-perf. building and blueprinting one of the most popular two stroke engines. Includes: Two cycle engine basics • Blueprinting and tuning the entire engine • Tips for ultimate power • Building for reliability • Complete engine machining • Ignition system • Carburetor tips • Using alcohol • Expansion chamber and exhaust tuning • Maintenance. Full of photos. **#S151 ..... $9.95**

How To Run A Successful Racing Business

How to operate a racing-oriented business successfully. How to: Start a business • Put more profit in a business • Cost controls • Proper advertising • Dealing with employees, taxes, and accountants • And much more. The secrets of business fundamentals and how to make them work for you. For existing businesses too. **#S143 . . . $9.95**

Racing The Small Block Chevy

A totally up-to-date high performance guide to the small block Chevy. Covers: High performance at a reasonable cost • Component blueprinting • Revealing cam, carb head porting and ignition tips from many of racing's best known engine builders • 330 illustrations. **#S112 . . . $9.95**

Buick Free Spirit Power Manual

Complete information on the performance engine of the future — the Buick V6. Blocks, crankshafts, rods, valve gear, intake and exhaust systems, ignition, susupension, brakes and body modifications. **All new** revised edition. Complete list of performance hardware. Over 200 photos and drawings. **#S123 ..... $9.95**

Complete Reference Guide

The "Yellow Pages" of the high performance world. Where to get: Hardware, chassis and engine parts, running gear, etc. Where to find: Fabricators, engine builders, safety gear, racing associations, driving schools, etc. A unique and valuable reference source for racers. 430 illus. **#S108 . . . $8.95**

Bob Bondurant High Perf Driving

A fascinating book that teaches the necessary skills for high-speed driving at minimum risk. Bondurant translates track-proven techniques into 12 chapters about getting the most out of yourself and your car and controlling it! Learn to do it from the master. Over 100 illus. 144 pages. **#MB35 . . . $11.95**

The Doctor's Guide To Automotive Ignition ✓ New!

The most complete book on high performance and automotive ignitions ever written. All about conventional and electronic ignitions. Includes: Hi performance from factory electronic ignitions • Improving engine and ignition performance • Creating custom tailored systems • Complete troubleshooting guide • Tech tips for ultimate ignition • and much more. **#J153 ... $12.95**

Practical Engine Swapping

Covers every swap problem, such as: Will it fit? • what's practical • buying an engine • where to buy hardware • steering and suspension alterations • making all linkages fit • building adaptors • solving oiling and electrical problems • and much, much more. **#S111 . . . $8.95**

Building The V6/Vega

The combination of Buick V6 in a Vega is a low-cost, easy-to-do project. It goes through the V6/Vega swap step by step, including mounts, wiring, exhaust, radiators, transmissions, and H.D. suspension. Which engines and which Vegas are best to use. With this book you can build the lowest cost, hardest running car in your county! **#S129 . . . $7.95**

Street Rod Builder's Notebook

An 8½ by 11 booklet which serves as a complete step-by-step planning guide, cost planner, and full specification sheet so you know exactly what went into your street rod. Indispensable! **#S136 . . . $4.95**

Street Rod Building Skills

This book will make a real street rod craftsman out of you! Contains details of methods and procedures long guarded by the "old timers" of the trade. Details such subjects as metal shrinking, hammer welding, working with wood for rods, upholstery and button tufting, how to do engine-turned gold leafing, pinstriping, and much, much more. Over 400 photos really give you the picture! **#S132 . . . $9.95**

How To Build A Repro Rod

An exciting new book which gives you all the skills and tools to tackle the job of rod building. Includes info on: frames • front and rear suspensions • drivetrain and engines • cooling • wheels and tires • brakes • body • wiring • plumbing • paint • upholstery • registration • insurance • suppliers list. The complete proven plan for building a rod. **#S134 . . . $9.95**

Guide To Fabricating Shop Equipment

Would you believe an engine stand, hydraulic press, engine hoist, sheet metal brake and motorized flame cutter all for under $400? It's true. Step-by-step instructions and concise photos and drawings show you how to easily construct them yourself. **#S145 ...... $9.95**

New! Trailers — How To Buy & Evaluate New! ✓

A complete guide to: Buying a used or new trailer • Designing and engineering a trailer for your use • Trailer components, tongues, couplers, the right hitch • Selecting the right tires • Creating towability • Eliminating sway • Trailer brakes, suspension, stability. Well illustrated. **#S150 ..... $9.95**

New! How To Build a SuperStreet New! and Bracket Racer

A complete all-encompassing book for the stock racer from basics to building. Includes: Traction and weight transfer • Rear suspension systems • Building and preparing your racer system by system: body, driveshaft, rear end, clutch and trans, automatic trans, brakes, tires, safety hardware, fuels and lubricants, supercharging, nitrous oxide. Includes tips on driving and bracket racing strategy. Plus, information to fully prepare and build your engine. And much, much more. Packed with photos. **#S149 ..... $11.95**